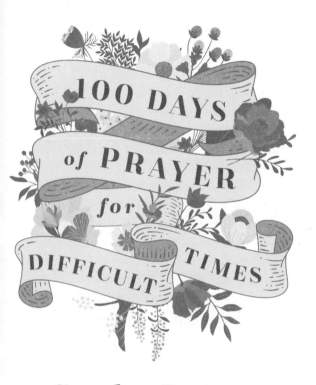

100 DAYS of PRAYER for DIFFICULT TIMES

Carolyn Larsen

Revell
a division of Baker Publishing Group
Grand Rapids, Michigan

© 2023 by Carolyn Larsen

Published by Revell
a division of Baker Publishing Group
PO Box 6287, Grand Rapids, MI 49516-6287
www.revellbooks.com

Printed in the United States of America

Library of Congress Cataloging-in-Publication Data
Names: Larsen, Carolyn, 1950- author.
Title: 100 days of prayer for difficult times / Carolyn Larsen.
Other titles: One hundred days of prayer for difficult times
Description: Grand Rapids : Revell, a division of Baker Publishing Group, [2023] | Includes index.
Identifiers: LCCN 2022031018 | ISBN 9780800740832 (cloth) | ISBN 9781493441358 (ebook)
Subjects: LCSH: Prayers. | Consolation.
Classification: LCC BV245 .L265 2023 | DDC 242/.8—dc23/eng/20220630
LC record available at https://lccn.loc.gov/2022031018

Baker Publishing Group publications use paper produced from sustainable forestry practices and post-consumer waste whenever possible.

23 24 25 26 27 28 29   7 6 5 4 3 2 1

Introduction

Dear gentle reader,

These last couple of years have been *difficult* . . . hence the name for this book of prayers. I suppose Covid started the spiral into struggle, fear, despair, hope, then struggle again. But other things willingly jumped on the bandwagon: a broken relationship with someone I love very much; retirement and moving to a new state, which, yes, has its good points, but also meant leaving behind old friends, hobbies, and activities I enjoyed very much; my aging body announcing that we'd no longer be participating in certain sports; saying goodbye to a church my family had been part of for over forty years. All of that comes under the heading of "Change," which is never easy.

3

As I've thought about my struggles and where to find a new pathway forward, the gift of prayer has shone brightly in my darkness. God invites us to come to him and tell him what's on our hearts and what floods our thoughts at 3:00 a.m. (Seriously, 3:00 nearly every dark morning, my mind will jump to "what if" scenarios.) He invites our prayers simply because he cares. Isn't that amazing? The God of the universe, the God of all things, cares about my piddly problems—because they are not piddly to me. He patiently listens as I pray, even though sometimes my prayers are a laundry list of what I want him to do and how he should "fix" things. Sometimes my prayers are cries of despair. But, oh yes, sometimes they are declarations of submission and trust because I know—I believe—that he can do something about the situations and that he will, even if it isn't what I think he should do. He listens to my prayers because he cares.

I also think about the privilege of praying for others' needs. It brings to mind the childhood game of Red Rover. Did you ever play that? Teammates clasp hands, forming a hopefully unbreakable chain so that when an opponent runs full speed at the chain, trying to break through, the chain stands strong. Sure, their arms may get bruised and sometimes the chain breaks, but the goal is—TOGETHER WE ARE STRONG. I see the privilege of praying with friends and for friends as a Red Rover kind of prayer experience. We are joined by our concern for the situation or person we pray for. Together we bring our intercession to God. We are joined together by our care. Together we are strong.

Perhaps you have a specific prayer need. Check out the index of topics in the back of this book. One of these prayers may help you jump-start your conversation with God. Read these prayers through the filter of your own relationship with the God who cares and in the midst of your own difficult times. I pray you find comfort and the assurance of God's answer as you come to a humble submission to his will. Together we are strong, so "Red Rover, Red Rover, send problems right over," because God cares.

Blessings,
Carolyn

1

When You're Barely Hanging On

Dear God,
I pray for women today who are holding on to the wildly frayed ends of their ropes. I've been there many times and probably will be again at some point. I pray for their weary hearts to be focused solidly on you, Jesus. Give each one a true awareness of your presence with them through the chaos that is their life right now. Give them more than just the head knowledge

of your presence. Instead, give them an intense visceral sense deep in their hearts that you've got their backs, you're giving them strength, and you're guiding their steps, and that means they are not alone. I pray for your power in their hearts to shut down Satan's efforts to cause doubt, confusion, or hopelessness, because that evil being will be relentless with those thoughts.

Oh loving, powerful God, remind these dear ones that they are truly never alone. And with that knowledge, give them confidence to get up every day and do what they must do with the assurance that you are in front of them, beside them, and behind them. Only you can help them through these days, Lord. I know. I've been there.

---

*I know the LORD is always with me.
I will not be shaken, for he is right
beside me.*

Psalm 16:8

2

Battling the Worry Monster

Dear Father,

Sometimes I facetiously quip that worrying is my spiritual gift. I know it isn't actually funny though. I humbly confess that too often I worry instead of trusting you, and then I worry more because I know I'm not trusting you. Worry feels like an endless loop. It doesn't seem to take much these days to send me over the edge. I have trouble settling my heart on something that brings peace and keeping it there. I need you, Lord. I need to know . . . to actually believe . . . that you aren't surprised by anything that's happening in my life. I need to know . . . to truly trust . . . that you see the road ahead and you already know how things will turn out. I need to know . . . well, I do already know . . . that you love me more than I can possibly imagine. I just forget that truth once in a while. Help me focus on your love. Help me find peace in your love. Help me push worry away so there is room in my heart to trust your love.

Don't fret or worry. Instead of worrying, pray. Let petitions and praises shape your worries into prayers, letting God know your concerns. Before you know it, a sense of God's wholeness, everything coming together for good, will come and settle you down. It's wonderful what happens when Christ displaces worry at the center of your life.

Philippians 4:6–7 The Message

3

Growing through Problems

Loving Father,
I know I'm supposed to appreciate the challenges I'm facing these days. I guess I should be celebrating them because, through them, my faith has the opportunity to grow stronger as I learn to lean on you and trust you. Of course, I want a deeper, stronger faith, but I have to be honest. My heart is bruised and battered, so I don't feel very strong right now. However, I don't want to miss out on the opportunity for

faith growth, so all I can do is ask for your help. Father, I ask you to give me strength. Please, fill my heart with your strength and power. Help me recognize the good lessons I'm learning through these struggles. Help me appreciate the growth and maturity that will come from this as I stay close to you and stay true to you. You know how I struggle. You know my weakness. But you also know that, even in the midst of the pain, I truly long to grow into an ever-deepening relationship with you.

Oh precious Lord, be patient with me and help me to be patient with myself as I learn, a step at a time, to hang on tightly to you and your Word through difficult times. Celebrate with me that my faith muscle is growing stronger with each bruise and wince of pain. I celebrate all I'm learning through these tests!

My friends, be glad, even if you have a lot of trouble. You know you learn to endure by having your faith tested.

James 1:2–3 CEV

4

Death Is Not the End

Oh Lord,

I'm grieving today. My precious friend just took her last breath on this earth. But even in my grief, I choose to celebrate because I know that this was not the end for her since she belongs to you! Thank you, Father, that even though my heart is breaking today because I have said goodbye to my friend, I am assured that we will have a future "hello" because Jesus said that he *is* the resurrection and the life and that anyone who believes in him will not die.

I am your daughter and so is my friend, so we will be reunited in heaven one day! What joy there is to know that today's goodbye is not forever. It's only a pause until I see my friend again in your glorious heaven. And it's even more wonderful that neither of us will know any pain—physical or emotional—in our eternity with you. We will have no problems and no trouble. Life with you will be a glorious celebration forever and ever. And what joy to know that as my friend closed her eyes to life on this earth today, when she opened them again she was in your presence! Thank you, Lord, that this is not the end. It's not the end. It is a glorious, wonderful, eternal beginning.

Jesus told her, "I am the resurrection and the life. Anyone who believes in me will live, even after dying."

John 11:25

5

Following My Leader

Dear loving Father,

I love the words of Deuteronomy 31:8 because they tell me that you're walking ahead of me, clearing the bushes and branches of the jungle, swinging a scythe to chop away the weeds and vines with which Satan tries to entangle me. You are the Waymaker. You are the Path Clearer. You are the Scout going before me. I don't need to be afraid because you already know what's ahead. You may not change what I'm going to face, but you're preparing me to handle it. I know that I may not see the entire cleared path because you may show me only one cleared step at a time. However, I know that I am not going through the jungle alone. You're leading me every step of the way, just as you always have been.

Father, I'm going to visualize putting my hand on your shoulder as you lead the way. I will step into the footprints you have made. I trust that you will not let me get lost along the way. Help me, encourage me, strengthen me as I make every effort not to doddle behind you with complaints and fears. Help me, Father, not to be afraid but to always stay close to you, knowing you will lead me to safety and peace.

Do not be afraid or discouraged, for the LORD *will personally go ahead of you. He will be with you; he will neither fail you nor abandon you.*

Deuteronomy 31:8

6

Step by Step

My patient Father,

I confess that I'm a slow learner. Time and time again I've seen you work miracles in the most difficult situations. Big miracles and small miracles (is there really a "small" miracle?). I've sensed your comforting presence when I have been in deep pain. I've heard your gentle voice say, "Be patient, child. This is step one. I'm not finished with your journey." Yet here I am, once again facing a painful crisis, and just like so many times before, I couldn't sleep last night. In my wakefulness I agonized about what *could* happen. I planned out strategies in my mind to handle the "what if" situations. I practiced conversations I might have with the people involved, and I . . . need to just stop.

I honestly do believe that no problem is too big for you, so why can't I remember that you will always, always, always show up for me? I know you love me more than I can begin to understand. Please, help me stop worrying and give me the strength to focus on step one—the here and now—and to patiently wait for step two. Oh Father, I will give you the credit for every step along the way.

You are my strong shield,
and I trust you completely.
You have helped me,
and I will celebrate
and thank you in song.
Psalm 28:7 CEV

7

Good and Perfect Gifts

Dear Father,

I'm more aware than ever today of the many ways you take care of me. And I just want to say that I am grateful. So very grateful. Some days I feel like I'm in the center of a dark, dark cloud. There's no light guiding me and I have little hope of things getting better. Oh God, you understand what a heavy heart feels like. You see the powerful effort it takes to get up, get dressed, and go about the obligations of the day. And you provide the strength I need.

I'm not saying that you aren't enough for me, God, because I know I wouldn't make it through a single day without the assurance of your presence, strength, and love. But you lovingly provide above and beyond by sending a phone call from a friend or a visit from a neighbor with a bouquet of flowers. Or a meetup with my bestie for a good heart-to-heart chat. Or a cardinal on my patio. I know all those things are from you. I just want to say thank you, Father, for knowing what will encourage me—moment by moment. Thank you for knowing when I need a smile, a conversation, or just a small connection with the world around me and sending it. You're awesome. I love you.

Every good and perfect gift is from above, coming down from the Father of the heavenly lights, who does not change like shifting shadows.

James 1:17 NIV

8

Never Alone

My loving, caring Father,
You have not promised to take away hard things or to free me from the problems of human life or even to prevent me from experiencing crises, struggles, or disappointments. You have not promised a trouble-free life. You *have* promised that I will never face any of those things alone. You *have* promised that your presence— your Spirit—will go before me, be close behind me, and on either side. That means I am always surrounded by your presence that offers me strength and courage.

Father, your Word tells me that if I stay close to you and trust you when I'm going through difficult times, my faith can grow stronger. Trusting you will show me over and over again that you are with me, and that means I'll never have to face more than I can handle . . . even if it feels like it sometimes. I can survive a difficult crisis because I know the situation has not surprised you and you will never leave me but will be with me every step of the way. I will be a better woman, a better Christian, a better friend to others because of this experience.

I look behind me and you're there,
*   then up ahead and you're there,*
*   too—*
*   your reassuring presence, coming and*
*   going.*
This is too much, too wonderful—
*   I can't take it all in!*

Psalm 139:5–6 *The Message*

9

Simply Trust

Sovereign God,
The thing about painful, stressful times in life is that I don't know how long they'll last. So right now, I'm staring into a black hole of relationship problems that brings pain, uncertainty, and confusion. It could go on for a long time and that scares me. It's no secret that I don't make the best decisions when I'm faced with hard things in my life. Stress eating is my norm and that's not good. I just want the pain to be over. Sometimes I do remember to pray for your help. Well, to be honest, I usually just tell you how I want you to solve the crisis or make the pain go away.

Why can't I just trust that you will handle things? After all, your Word tells me you love me. Why is it so hard to trust you? I can look back at my experiences and see many times when you've protected me, guided me, and answered my prayers. It's not like there's no evidence of your power and your plan. Oh God, I humbly ask you to forgive my constant struggle to trust you. Please grow my trust in you and deepen my faith in your love for me.

Blessed is the man who trusts in the LORD,
*   whose trust is the LORD.*
He is like a tree planted by water,
*   that sends out its roots by the stream,*
and does not fear when heat comes,
*   for its leaves remain green,*
and is not anxious in the year of drought,
*   for it does not cease to bear fruit.*

Jeremiah 17:7–8 ESV

10

Listening for Your Voice

Precious Father,

I'm holding on to the truth that in the cacophony of voices racing through my mind and heart, yours is there. I want to hear it over the other noises, so I'll follow Jesus's example and move to a quiet place. I will be alone with you. I'll strive to be quiet and listen for your voice, my Shepherd, the One I trust. Oh Father, I ask for your help in pushing aside all the other voices shouting for my attention, telling me to doubt you, to be afraid, to be hopeless. They are lies, Father. I know they are lies.

Oh God, help me to step away from the things causing this anguish. Help me to quiet my heart and quiet my thoughts. Help me to be still as I sit near you. Speak words of comfort and strength into my soul. Give me reminders of your presence. I know that none of these painful, troubling things I'm going through have caught you off guard, and I do believe you have a plan in all this. I just need to be still and listen for your voice and no other voice. You will guide me, comfort me, give me wisdom. You are my all-powerful, mighty, loving God.

Be still, and know that I am God!

Psalm 46:10

11

Your Constant Presence

Oh Father,
One of the hardest things about being in a diffi-cult situation is the frightening feeling that I'm alone . . . the feeling that no one understands or empathizes with what I'm going through or that they don't even want to make the effort to care about me. I try to be careful not to talk too much about my problems or even my feel-ings because I am afraid my friends get tired of hearing about them. It's an isolating, lonely feeling. That makes me even more thankful

for the reminders that you are always with me. You know what's happening and you care. That helps a lot. I close my eyes and picture you watching over me just like a mother hen watching over her chicks, protecting, guiding, feeding. I remember that I'm never really alone because you are always here with me. Even when I'm scared. Even when I'm lonely. Even when I can't really sense your presence. You are here. You care. You love. You protect. You see what's ahead, and you're ready for it. I need your presence and protection, Lord. I'm forever grateful for it.

The LORD watches over you—
the LORD is your shade at your right
hand;
the sun will not harm you by day,
nor the moon by night.

Psalm 121:5–6 NIV

12

Help to Control Anger Issues

Dear God,

I'm finally facing this mess I've created. I know that I am often my own worst enemy. I unintentionally create chaos in my life by how I speak to and behave toward others. I confess that I have an out-of-control hot temper and that I've used the "that's just how I am" excuse way too often. However, it's time for me to admit what that means. When I fly off the handle at someone, my temper lays the groundwork for the difficult situation and damaged relationship that develops. Of course, I don't want to be a doormat for others by letting them walk all over me. But I admit that my anger has never yet solved any issue . . . only made things worse.

Father, I need your help to control my anger. Teach me how to respond to others with strength but still be respectful. Show me how to stand up for myself but be understanding of others' opinions and feelings. Help me learn to defuse a difficult situation right at the beginning rather than escalate it with my attitude and words. Father, I want to reflect you in every situation. I am your woman. Help me act like it.

A hot-tempered person starts fights;
a cool-tempered person stops them.
Proverbs 15:18

13

Saving Relationships

Oh God,
I humbly ask that you hear the cry of my heart. Only you can soften the hearts and restore the relationships that appear to be hopelessly broken in this situation.

Father, I pray that just as you did for Saul on the Damascus road, you will open eyes, hearts, and minds so that the dear ones involved can see—really see—who you are and what you desire for them in these relationships. You did a miracle in Saul's life and I'm asking for one now, Lord. Help them see what's at stake by their attitudes and behaviors—relationships lost, loved ones left behind, and lives damaged. Guide them to think about their words before speaking them and to be respectful to loved ones who have different opinions or attitudes. Respect doesn't cost anything. These relationships will only change through the miracle of your intervening power.

Oh God, I know you have the power to change hearts, to open eyes, to clear minds, to lift the blinding scales caused by deception. I ask you to intervene. May these dear ones know that their salvation in this is only by your incredible power and intense love working for them and through them.

Lord God, you stretched out your mighty arm and made the sky and the earth. You can do anything.

Jeremiah 32:17 CEV

14

God's Incredibly Persistent Love

My God,

Nothing is too hard for you. No situation is too overwhelming. No mountain is too big. No ocean is too deep. You can put Satan in his place. You can change a person's stone-cold heart. You can open someone's tightly clenched eyes so they can see your love. You are my powerful God, and you love me more than I can fathom. Nothing can separate me from your love. Nothing and no one can turn you away from me. You promised never to leave me, no matter what happens. What comfort there is in that, Father. I can know peace because of that truth. I don't have to stress about anything because you will handle all the things that life throws at me. You have a plan for me and you're already working things out, step by step. I know that any worry or anxiety is just a waste of time. I choose to trust you and wait on your guidance and answers. I may need to make that choice many times a day. But I will—as many times as necessary—because you are my God and nothing can change your love for me. Thank you!

I'm absolutely convinced that nothing— nothing living or dead, angelic or demonic, today or tomorrow, high or low, thinkable or unthinkable—absolutely nothing can get between us and God's love because of the way that Jesus our Master has embraced us.

Romans 8:38–39 *The Message*

15

New Stage of Life

Dear Father,

I'm in a season of change, and for the most part, it's changing because of things outside of my control. I might be transitioning into some good new things, but I'm not sure yet. It's difficult because I don't yet know what I'm transitioning to. I only know what I'm leaving behind. And, truth be told, I really liked what was back there. Of course, this change is not easy because I got comfortable in the "what is" and didn't think at all about the "what's next."

Anyway, here I stand at the doorway of something new, and I confess that I'm pretty scared. I ask that you give me courage to keep facing forward, anticipating the new instead of looking back at the old. I trust that you still have a purpose for me. I just need to wait for the "what's next" to be revealed. Well, you know how good I am at waiting (not at all). Still, you've promised to be with me each day of my life. You've given me talents, abilities, and passions and the energy to pursue them. Some of those things have changed over the years, but that just helps me know that new things will still come. So, in this stressful time, Father, I wait. I trust. I anticipate. I submit. I celebrate your plan and your love.

Being confident of this, that he who began a good work in you will carry it on to completion until the day of Christ Jesus.

Philippians 1:6 NIV

16

Longing
for Peace

Oh my loving Father,
My heart longs for peace. I'm so tired of being anxious. I'm tired of being confused. While it's true that life is throwing some messy curves in my direction right now, I think I've been concentrating too much attention and emotional energy on the problems instead of on you. I continually think about the "what ifs" or what might possibly happen and that keeps my mind and heart captured in fear and darkness.

Oh God, when my thoughts get stuck on those scary possibilities, remind me . . . help me . . . turn them to your promises that you will be with me, protect me, guide me, and work things out. You are the place of peace. You are the keeper of peace. I'm certain I will not find peace until I trust you and focus on you. I know you will walk with me every moment because you love me. I know you have a plan for my future. Even though I can't see what the end is going to look like, I know that you can, so I must trust you. I don't want some kind of half-hearted trust, Father. Help me to trust you, moment by moment. I realize it's a choice to do so, but I will not find peace anywhere else.

Thank you for your love. Thank you that I can trust you with my life, health, relationships . . . everything. Thank you for peace.

You will keep in perfect peace
all who trust in you,
all whose thoughts are fixed on you!

Isaiah 26:3

17

Choosing to Believe

Dear Father,

There are days when I cannot feel your presence. Even on those days, I choose to believe that you are with me. Belief is stronger than feeling. I believe that, regardless of how insurmountable my problems seem, you are stronger. I believe that even when life surprises me with roadblocks and speed bumps, you are not surprised. I believe that even when I feel alone and scared, your love is still surrounding me. Your Word tells me over and over that your love is constant, strong, powerful, and unchanging. Your Word tells me that nothing can come between your love and me. Your love is forever. I choose to believe in your love even when Satan tells me that it's a lie.

Father, whatever this day may bring, I choose to believe that your incredible love is surrounding me, protecting me, and guiding me. I choose to say thank you for your presence. Thank you for your wisdom. Thank you for your grace. Thank you for not giving up on me when my faith wavers, because sometimes it does. Most of all, thank you for your love that I know will never let me go.

Praise God in heaven!
God's love never fails.
Psalm 136:26 CEV

18

Praying in Darkness

Almighty Lord,

The hardest part of standing by and watching a loved one struggle with something is not knowing what's actually happening or what the future will hold. I don't want to be intrusive in her life, and I do understand that her first priority is not rushing to tell me what's happening. But Father, it's hard to care about someone and know they are hurting but not know how things are (or are not) progressing as I pray.

Sometimes I feel like I'm praying in darkness because I don't know what to pray. I do take great comfort in the fact that you know everything that's going on. So even when I don't know how to pray, you know my heart desires the best for my loved one. I'm grateful that you already know what the future holds and you love the people involved even more than I do. You know what's best for all. I ask that you guide my loved one's thoughts, actions, words . . . every step she takes. Keep her close to you. Comfort her and strengthen her. Give her a good future and a constant hope. I'm thankful that I don't have to know everything because I trust the One who does.

"I know the plans I have for you," says the Lord. "They are plans for good and not for disaster, to give you a future and a hope."

Jeremiah 29:11

19

God's Amazing Grace

My loving Father,
It is only by your grace that I get through each day. When life gets so heavy that it presses me to the ground, your grace lifts me up. When the anxiety of dealing with things alone makes me afraid, your grace gives me courage. When the uncertainty of the future overwhelms me, your grace gives me peace.

Your precious grace, Father, is completely undeserved yet so freely given. Your grace knows that my heart wants to trust you completely and understands that sometimes I fail miserably. Your grace knows that sometimes doubts and fears are my weak humanness overriding my faith . . . and by your grace, you forgive me. Your grace reaches out to me, constantly whispering that things will be okay and that I only need to believe. It is only by your grace that I even know you. Your grace provided salvation. Your grace promises heaven. It is because of your grace that I have hope that the future will be better than the now. Your grace promises me there will be even more purpose in my future days . . . because, by your grace, you have a plan for my life, not just today but in every day to come. I'm thankful for your grace.

Let us come boldly to the throne of our gracious God. There we will receive his mercy, and we will find grace to help us when we need it most.

Hebrews 4:16

20

The Gift of Other Christians

My gracious Father,

Some days I feel like I could take on anything the world tosses at me and I would easily win. Then some days I can barely drag myself out of bed. Depression overwhelms me, saps my energy . . . defeats me. I try to fight it, but I simply don't have the energy. Those difficult days are when I am so thankful for the encouragers, the friends, the challengers you've put in my life. I know beyond a shadow of a doubt that you *placed* these specific people near me. They intentionally remind me of your love for me. They recall your strength and power for me. They talk about your constant presence with me and will not let me forget it.

These dear ones, Father, are your ambassadors to me. They are your followers, witnessing of your love, power, presence, and plan. They pick me up when I can't pick myself up. They sing my song of worship to you when I can't remember the words. It is through them that I regain my faith footing. It is with their help that I am pulled back to you.

Thank you for them. Thank you for their courage in speaking words of challenge and faith to bring me back to a place of hope and trust. They are your gift to me in my darkest times.

Two people are better off than one, for they can help each other succeed. If one person falls, the other can reach out and help. But someone who falls alone is in real trouble.

Ecclesiastes 4:9–10

21

Expect Difficult Times

Oh Father,

I'm going to be totally honest here—I wish you'd just take away times of pain and difficulty. How wonderful it would be if people who don't know you could look at my life and see that it's problem-free and smooth sailing. I promise I'd give you all the credit! All right, I know that isn't going to happen. In fact, you made it clear in your Word that life would definitely be hard at times. You even said to expect that. Some troubles are because of choices I've made. Some are because of choices others have made. Some are even because of my faith in you.

Thank you for helping me through each day by guiding my steps and even my thoughts. Thank you for giving me strength and courage to get up and face each day. Thank you that because of my trust in you, I can have peace in the midst of chaos. Thank you that you will help my faith grow stronger and deeper because of difficult times. Hard times aren't wasted with you because I always learn more about you and about my faith. Thank you that others can see your power and love as they see my peace in the middle of chaos. Father, may the way I make my journey show your presence and love to others.

I have told you this, so that you might have peace in your hearts because of me. While you are in the world, you will have to suffer. But cheer up! I have defeated the world.

John 16:33 CEV

22

Defusing Anger

Father,

I don't understand how Christians can treat other Christians so unkindly. I'm sorry, but I am pretty angry about what's going on. I'm angry that people I care about are suffering—not because of anything they have actually done but because of the assumptions of others. I'm angry that I can't fix it. I'm frustrated that you aren't fixing it. I'm sorry for that frustration. I understand that you must have a purpose in this, and I do want my faith and trust in you to grow. But the truth is that the ugly things being said in person and posted on social media—

well, they really hurt. All the people involved in this mess are Christians, so why is there so much disrespect and unkindness to one another? Why can't brothers and sisters in Christ forgive and move forward? I admit that I'm as guilty as anyone, so I'm really not throwing stones at others.

Father, help me to get past my anger. Teach me to control what I say—and to whom. Help me to forgive. Help me to make the first move toward reconciliation. Help me to show your love by my behavior and speech. And I pray for other Christians who are struggling with these same behaviors. Father, teach us kindness and respect, and show us that anger accomplishes nothing.

---

*A gentle response defuses anger,
but a sharp tongue kindles a
temper-fire.*

Proverbs 15:1 *The Message*

23

Building Strength

Father God,

Thank you for your constant presence in my life. Thank you that I will never need to face hard times in life alone. Thank you for your strength, so willingly and generously given to me. Thank you for your patience with me as I too often waffle between trust and worry. Thank you for reaching a hand down to rescue me when I'm sinking into worry and panic. Thank you for your deep peace when I finally hold on to you tightly. Thank you that when I truly trust you during any struggle I face, my faith will grow stronger. Thank you that you already know how things are going to turn out. Thank you for caring enough about me to want to help me grow, even when it's painful. Thank you for your wisdom that guides me to know what to do and even what to say (when I listen to you). Thank you for friends who lift me up when I don't know how to stand. Thank you for the beauty of creation that reminds me of you. Thank you for . . . you.

We can rejoice, too, when we run into problems and trials, for we know that they help us develop endurance. And endurance develops strength of character, and character strengthens our confident hope of salvation.

Romans 5:3–4

24

You Helped Me Make It

Oh God,

I'm still here! I just went through the hardest, most painful, scariest thing I could have imagined, and I'M. STILL. HERE! There were times I thought I wouldn't survive, but I did. There were days when I thought I'd lose my mind, but I didn't. Some weeks I thought I'd been abandoned and was alone, but I wasn't! Day by day—no, minute by minute—I just cried out to you, my precious Father. You helped me push myself to stand and put one foot in front of the other and do what I had to do. Every minute. Every hour. Every day. And I'm still here! I made it through.

Looking in the rearview mirror, I see time after time when you held me, strengthened me, guided my steps, pulled my thoughts toward you. That's how I know I would not have made it if not for you. I was never alone. When I needed strength and courage, you gave it. Now I know I can face anything that may come in the future, because I've seen what you will do and I know I can trust you.

He will feed his flock like a shepherd.
He will carry the lambs in his arms,
holding them close to his heart.
He will gently lead the mother sheep
with their young.

Isaiah 40:11

25

Secure in God's Love

Oh God,

You took my breath away. In the day-after-day grayness of my struggles, you pulled back a curtain and the light and power of your love flooded my soul, blinded my eyes, and warmed my aching heart. Sweet light. Sweet love. Sweet presence. I confess that I needed the reminder, Father. I know you never leave me, but sometimes I need a glimpse of light and hope, like the sun breaking through dark clouds, even if just for a moment. Now I can take a deep breath and hang on to the hope and trust I have in you the next time trouble comes.

I'm thankful there are still surprises in our long-term relationship, Lord. I'm thankful that my understanding of you grows beyond the boundaries I've unintentionally set. You are bigger, stronger, more powerful, more grace-giving, more loving, more intentional than I can ever understand. Nothing—absolutely nothing—can take you away from me. What a blessing that is. So, filled with the beauty of today's surprise, I cling to you with all my heart.

Can anything ever separate us from Christ's love? Does it mean he no longer loves us if we have trouble or calamity, or are perse-cuted, or hungry, or destitute, or in danger, or threatened with death? . . . No, despite all these things, overwhelming victory is ours through Christ, who loved us.

Romans 8:35, 37

26

I Need Help to Trust

Father,

I'm scared. I'm so scared that I'm doubting your care, your protection, even your love. Fear is welling up in my heart. It's overwhelming my thoughts. Anxiety wakes me from sleep, creeps in to interrupt my prayers, and even takes over my mind when I read Scripture, pushing your truths aside. I can't seem to get on top of it, Lord. I try. I really do. I give my troubles to you and have about thirty seconds of peace before the fear explodes inside me again.

Oh Lord, I long for the peace that can come only from you. I long for the strength to let go of my control issues and trust you with everything. Trusting you is the only way I can make it. You're the only one who can handle this situation. Father, I know that fear and love can't occupy the same space, so I ask you to take away my doubt and fear. Guide me in how to rest in your love and peace. My faith is weak, Lord. Help me trust you. Trust you. Trust you.

I cried out, "I am slipping!"
   but your unfailing love, O Lord,
      supported me.
When doubts filled my mind,
   your comfort gave me renewed hope
      and cheer.

Psalm 94:18–19

27

Your Word Promises Hope

My sovereign God,
Sometimes situations seem hopeless. Relationships appear beyond repair. Finances are tenuous. Oh Father, I know that hope comes only from you and through you. In the still, dark hours of the night, when worry and fear threaten to blanket me, it's because of you that I have hope to keep going. Hope that things will get better eventually. Hope that together we will make it through. Hope that is promised in your Word because of your wisdom,

strength, and grace. I have hope only because I have you. I can hope because you know the end from the beginning and this mess in the middle is nothing to you. You have a plan for my life and nothing can change it. You are stronger and wiser than anything or anyone else in this world. Your Word tells me all of that and I trust it, so I have hope. Hope is trust with its work clothes on. Thank you for all the promises shared in your Word. Thank you for the hope for a better tomorrow.

I pray that God, the source of hope, will fill you completely with joy and peace because you trust in him. Then you will overflow with confident hope through the power of the Holy Spirit.

Romans 15:13

28

Victory over Death

My Father God,

I want to thank you for giving me a much needed perspective change. My instinctive reaction to loss or even to change is worry and grief. But you've opened my eyes to a different way of thinking about the difficult things that inevitably come in life . . . a hopeful way. You've reminded me that death is part of life. Oh, I don't necessarily mean physical death, though I know that's certainly a part of life too. You've reminded me that I will inevitably face many kinds of death: death of a job or career, death of a relationship or friendship, and even death of a dream. But, praise God, at the heart of any death there is Jesus's promise of new life because he is the resurrection *and* the life. There is victory through hope! The eye-opening thing for me is that death of the old must happen in order to make room for the new. Thank you for reminding me of this, Father. Now when I face painful times of change in my life, instead of complaining or worrying, I will excitedly anticipate the newness you will bring.

For everything there is a season,
a time for every activity under heaven.

Ecclesiastes 3:1

29

Surrendering to Your Will

My loving Father,
It's time to be honest with you . . . and with myself. I spend a lot of my prayer time complaining about how difficult life is. I *tell* you how to make things better for me. I apparently think I have answers that are better than yours. I act like I'm a victim in any scenario that isn't playing out the way I want it to. But the honest truth is that my difficulties, my situations, are usually because of my own behavior and choices. I do things my way, even when I know it's not

the best choice, then I come crying to you and expect you to fix it. You, in your grace and love, always redirect me onto a good track. But I can be a slow learner, God, and it's not long before I'm back in a tough situation . . . all caused by my own actions.

Father, the truth is . . . I'm tired. I'm tired of the struggle. I'm tired of the fight. I'm tired of not being in tune with you because of my own stubbornness and unwillingness to submit to your guidance and wisdom. I sincerely ask you to forgive me, Lord. When I recklessly push for my own way, remind me of the past struggles I've caused myself and that every single one of those times I've come to realize later that your way is best. It's always best.

Surrender to God! Resist the devil, and he will run from you.

James 4:7 CEV

30

Teach Me to Wait

My patient Father,
I confess to you that I am an arrogant and impatient woman. When I ask for your help with a problem, I want an immediate response with a complete answer. That's what I want, but you don't do what I want because you have something better in mind for me.

As I look back over my life and the times I've prayed for your help, I see that your answers most often come one step at a time. That means my strength and growth have come a step at a time, usually after a lot of complaining. In my impatience, I want the whole answer immediately, but of course, no faith is required for that.

Thank you for caring about me enough to want my faith to grow stronger and deeper. Thank you for doing what's necessary to help that happen. I appreciate the faith-muscle stretches that teach me and grow me. I honestly do not want the easy way out, Father. I want to be willing to go through deep waters, even when it's painful and difficult. I want the experiences that will teach me and stretch my faith and grow me into the woman you see when you look at me. Teach me to wait and to trust so that my faith can grow and mature.

They who wait for the LORD shall renew
*   their strength;*
*   they shall mount up with wings like*
*   eagles;*
they shall run and not be weary;
*   they shall walk and not faint.*

Isaiah 40:31 ESV

31

New Life in Jesus

Dear Father,

I have accepted Jesus as my Savior, but I still live in this world, around the same people, in the same situations I had before accepting Jesus. However, the Bible tells me I am to be dead to this life. How do I do that, Father? Colossians 3:3 tells me that my new life is with Christ in God, so I must look beyond the circumstances of my day-in-and-day-out life and focus on knowing Jesus more and more.

Teach me as I study his life. Help me understand his words. Too often I am consumed with my struggles and I try to make Jesus fit into my world, which means I'm still living in this life—I haven't let go of it as instructed. I believe you have a plan for my life and that you will guide my steps. You will help me to let go of this life— the priorities I had before knowing Jesus. You will help me grow to become more like him. But this can't happen while I'm holding on to what was instead of reaching toward what can be.

Oh God, help me to keep my eyes locked on Jesus. Help me to see his love, his compassion, his wisdom and strength. Help me learn to be more like him so that the cares of this world fall away and I can find my new life in him.

You died to this life, and your real life is hidden with Christ in God.

Colossians 3:3

32

God's Riches Freely Given

Almighty Father,

It's humbling to admit this, but . . . I deserve nothing from you. Your grace to me is only because of your great love for me. Thank you for saving me, forgiving me, loving me. Thank you for hearing my prayers—not just hearing them but actually wanting me to tell you what's on my heart. Thank you for listening to me describe what I hope you will do and for caring how I feel about difficult times in my life.

I am amazed by your grace. Of course, you absolutely know what's best for me. You already know how you're going to deal with the situations I bring to you. I know that you already have a plan, but thank you for letting me bare my heart to you anyway. I do trust you to take care of me and protect me in your way and in your time. I truly believe that when all is said and done, I will be just fine because I've seen your powerful love and wise care in my history with you. Of course, that doesn't mean I'm not afraid sometimes. But I know that if I keep trusting you and depending on you, my faith will grow stronger. I'm not consistently good at that, but I'm learning. Thank you for giving me your grace. It has made my life with you possible.

God saved us and called us to live a holy life. He did this, not because we deserved it, but because that was his plan from before the beginning of time—to show us his grace through Christ Jesus.

2 Timothy 1:9

33

Getting past Worry

Oh God,

I worry about everything—money, not having food, not being able to pay my bills or get fuel for my car. I worry about broken relationships. I worry about losing my job. I know that my worry is actually a lack of trust, isn't it? It's a control issue, because I always want to have everything figured out. I like to know what's coming. But if I have everything figured out, then there's no room for faith. I've filled all available space in my mind and heart with worry or efforts to control.

Oh God, I want to be able to just trust. Why is it so hard? I know you've always taken care of me, and sometimes in surprising, even amazing, ways. Worry is so consuming. Help me to be able to let go and just watch what you do that shows me (and everyone else) that you are God and can handle anything!

Father, help me trust you for the long term, giving you the chance to work out your plan before I start screaming for you to do something!

Give your entire attention to what God is doing right now, and don't get worked up about what may or may not happen tomorrow. God will help you deal with whatever hard things come up when the time comes.

Matthew 6:34 *The Message*

34

Comfort in Constancy

Dear Father,

Things in this world are constantly changing. They change so quickly, I can't keep up with everything—styles, culture, laws, thoughts, even how we do church. It's kind of frightening.

It's so comforting that one thing never changes: Jesus. He is the same today as the day I first met him. You and Jesus loved me completely on that day. You love me today as much as yesterday and will still love me tomorrow.

His teachings are the same. He is steady and constant. His character isn't blown around by problems or people or politics or anything else. He is your Son, God, and you define yourself as love. You and Jesus are love. That love is directed at me. That means whatever problems I'm facing today, your love is walking with me, guiding me, protecting me, teaching me. Nothing can change that. Nothing will move you away from me.

Thank you that changes in this world don't change who you are or how you love me. My own doubts don't change any of that either. My fear doesn't make you panic. Thank you for being steady, constant, powerful, and loving— you always are.

Jesus Christ never changes! He is the same yesterday, today, and forever.

Hebrews 13:8 CEV

35

Forgiving as God Forgives

Loving God,

Life is not very pleasant right now. I'm angry and hurt because of the way I've been treated. I was treated badly! Unfairly! And I didn't deserve it. I didn't behave badly or say anything wrong or unkind. The treatment just came out of nowhere. I can't stop thinking about it. Do I want to get revenge? Yes, kind of . . . okay, a lot. I know I should forgive and move on. But, Father, she's not even sorry. It's like she doesn't care at all how much her words hurt. She says she's not responsible for my feelings. But what about her actions and words that precipitated my feelings? How do I forgive when there's no recognition of the hurt?

Oh God, I just realized what I said . . . and that you forgive me time after time, even when I won't admit what I've done. Even when I'm not really sorry. Even when . . . I know what I need to do, Father. But I need your help to let go of my anger and actually, truly forgive. I know that holding anger not only hurts me, it hurts others and hurts my life with you. Please, help me forgive and move on. Help me forgive, as you forgive me.

Be kind and compassionate to one another, forgiving each other, just as in Christ God forgave you.

Ephesians 4:32 NIV

36

Satan's Lies

Sovereign Lord,
More than ever before, I am aware of Satan's sneaky efforts to pull me away from you. He tries to discredit you and make me doubt you. He whispers that you don't really love me and that I don't matter to you or that you won't help me. He says you aren't strong enough to do anything. I know it's all lies. But he's so persistent and sneaky that sometimes what he says begins to make sense. He knows when I'm doubting and where I'm weak, and that's exactly where he strikes. I can picture him wandering back and forth just watching for a chance to attack.

Father, keep reminding me that you're close to me. Help me remember that you never leave me to fight Satan alone. I trust your presence. I know your strength—after all, you're the ruler of heaven's armies. Stronger than any other power. Wiser than any other being. You see the end from the beginning.

Oh God, wrap me in your arms; protect me from Satan's evil efforts. Keep my mind focused on you, trusting you. Hold me close so my heart stays centered on you. You are my protector. You are my guide. You are my strength. You are my courage. You are my wisdom. You are all I need.

Stay alert! Watch out for your great enemy, the devil. He prowls around like a roaring lion, looking for someone to devour.

1 Peter 5:8

37

Prayer Is Hard

Oh Father,

I'm so tired. I'm hurting. I'm confused. I'm scared and I just feel so alone. So many things in life are really hard right now. I'm not even sure how things got to this point. There doesn't seem to be anything I can do to make things better. I've tried. Believe me, I've tried. But to no avail. That means I can't do anything except pray, which, of course, is the best thing to do.

But God, I'm just going to be honest here—sometimes prayer is hard too because it feels like I'm just saying words and the prayers aren't even leaving the room. It *feels* like no one is listening. I know that's not true, of course. I know that's when faith comes in, isn't it? Those times when I struggle with prayer, I must lean on my faith and on your promises. I know that you promise to hear my prayers, so I will keep right on praying. You tell me to pray, so I will pray. You care about knowing what's on my heart, so I will pray. Even when I can't *feel* your presence, I know you're listening. I believe you. I trust you. So I will pray.

How bold and free we then become in his presence, freely asking according to his will, sure that he's listening. And if we're confident that he's listening, we know that what we've asked for is as good as ours.

1 John 5:14–15 The Message

38

No Fear

My precious Father,

Fear is taking over my thoughts and my heart. Fear that the people I love will be hurt. Fear that the situations we're facing will change life forever, and not in a good way. Fear that I'll be estranged from people I love.

Oh God, I ask for your strength to fight off the doubts and questions that fuel my sleeplessness. I ask for your strength to help me hang on to the truth that no situation surprises you. Nothing that's happening is out of your control. Your power and strength are greater than any human's attitude and choices or efforts to destroy.

Oh God, I pray for hearts to be softened toward others. I ask for God-given humility to shine through so that love can be restored. I pray for your will to be done. I pray for my own heart to be attuned to you, to trust you completely, and to love with abandon. I pray that you will help me see your guidance. Help me listen for you to tell me what to say and do. God, show me how to be your woman in my attitude toward everyone I meet. Thank you for your love, grace, and power.

Don't be afraid, for I am with you.
    Don't be discouraged, for I am your
      God.
I will strengthen you and help you.
    I will hold you up with my victorious
      right hand.

                     Isaiah 41:10

39

The Green-Eyed Monster

Father,

I've become aware of something that's both revealing and embarrassing. I have a habit of complaining about problems or struggles in my life. I blame other situations or people for problems I've created. I easily complain about unfairness. I loudly announce that troubles are piling up on me through what I say is no fault of my own. But I confess (and this isn't easy) that often my supposed problem or struggle is just that I'm jealous because another person got what I wanted and felt I deserved. Instead of congratulating and celebrating with that person, I let myself sink into a pity party like no other. I actually let the enemy bury me by filling my thoughts with ideas of persecution, or worse—invisibility—feeling that I've been overlooked or ignored. I even let myself dislike the person who got what I wanted.

I'm sorry. I really am. I don't like this side of me. I don't like that I allow this to happen. Forgive me, Father. Give me strength to fight off these feelings. Help me let go of my own ideas and just trust your plan for my life. Help me be patient to wait for my "next" to be revealed, regardless of how long that takes. And, Father, give me the strength of character to offer congratulations and celebrations to others . . . even when it hurts a little.

Wait for the LORD;
be strong, and let your heart take
courage;
wait for the LORD!

Psalm 27:14 ESV

40

Keep On Keeping On

Dear Father,

Some days I want to stay in bed, pull a blanket over my head, and just hide from life. I want to. But I know I can't. I realize that I can't quit just because something painful or difficult has developed. Hiding from the problem will not make it go away. In fact, it might make it worse. I have to get up and keep going. "Keep on keeping on" is what many would tell me.

But, oh God, sometimes it feels as though troubles pile one on top of the other. I feel weighted down, buried almost. It's hard to catch a deep breath. It's difficult to see light anywhere.

Still I know that none of what's happening surprises you. You see it all and . . . even when I feel like the load is just too heavy . . . you have purpose in everything that comes my way. Lessons to learn. Faith to build stronger. Trust to grow.

So, the "keep on keeping on" is important because of the things I'll learn that will make me a better woman and a more godly servant. I believe that nothing goes to waste with you. You will use every lesson I learn to grow me and to help me help others by what I learn. Give me strength to keep on keeping on, a step at a time, a day at a time, with my eyes focused on the goal of knowing and serving you!

I press on toward the goal for the prize of the upward call of God in Christ Jesus.

Philippians 3:14 ESV

41

High Hopes

Oh God,

I need hope. I know you see the brokenness in my life. I've made a real mess of things. Father, right now I need hope that my messes *can* be repaired. I cling to the hope of your promises—your love for me and for my future. Promises that you are working out the best things in my life and will carry out your plan for me. Thank you for the promise that if I keep my trust and hope in you, I will not be alone in this suffering.

I also need to own my responsibility in how I got to this place. Father, show me where I may be arrogant and proud. Show me where I have been hurtful and unkind. Let me see where I may have been dishonest or unfair. Give me the courage to confess and apologize so that the gateway to the hope of restoration can be opened.

My hope in your guidance and help is what keeps me grounded. Hope keeps me from giving up. Hope promises that you are paying attention and you have a plan. Hope means you see into the future—all the things to come that I have no clue about. Hope in you. Father, keep my hope strong and active!

God cannot tell lies! And so his promises and vows are two things that can never be changed.

We have run to God for safety. Now his promises should greatly encourage us to take hold of the hope that is right in front of us. This hope is like a firm and steady anchor for our souls. In fact, hope reaches behind the curtain and into the most holy place.

Hebrews 6:18–19 CEV

42

Be Still

My loving Father,

I have made myself sit in stillness this morning. It hasn't been easy, but I've allowed no distractions of screens or people or anything; it's been just me, my Bible, and you. I've kept my thoughts focused on you. When the enemy has tried to infiltrate, I've pushed him back and centered on you and your Word. And you know what? It's amazing that in a very few moments of keeping my heart intentionally settled on you and your Word, I heard you speak. I mean I almost heard you audibly speak, "Trust me, my child. Just trust me. Know my love for you is so deep and strong that nothing can break it. Nothing can take you away from me."

How precious you are, Father. How present, loving, and strong. In these few minutes of stillness, my peace has returned. I am assured of your care. I know I'm not alone. I believe that whatever this day or tomorrow or the day after that may hold, you will guide me through it. Thank you for your sweet voice assuring me of your love and care. I'll be all right now. I know it.

> "For even if the mountains walk away
>   and the hills fall to pieces,
> My love won't walk away from you,
>   my covenant commitment of peace
>   won't fall apart."
> The God who has compassion on you
>   says so.

Isaiah 54:10 The Message

43

Prayer for Peace in My Work Future

Dear Lord of peace,
I'm worried that I may be laid off from my job.
There have already been a few people let go.
I understand that some of the changes in our
world have created financial situations that are
causing the need for companies to downsize.
But the domino effect of that is problems for
people like me who have bills to pay. I don't
totally live paycheck to paycheck . . . but it's

close. Besides, I like my job. I try to be a good employee and coworker and do good work, but there is an undercurrent of fear among all of us these days. I can feel it.

Oh Father, calm my nerves. I know you have a plan for my life. None of the chaos in our world today has surprised you. And I know that if I do lose my job, you have a plan for something else for me. But it's hard not to worry. Forgive me for that, Father. Renew my trust in you. Help me remember how you have always taken care of me, often in ways I never would have expected. As peace returns to my heart, help me to have a calming effect on my coworkers. Father, help them to see that my trust in you is the reason I can have peace.

Now may the Lord of peace himself give you his peace at all times and in every situation. The Lord be with you all.

2 Thessalonians 3:16

44

Controlling My Thought Life

Father,

Thank you for reminding me of the importance of keeping my thought life under control. Too often I let my mind run to the dark corners of "What if this happens?" and all of a sudden, everything feels overwhelming. I've created scenarios that cause gigantic stresses and chaos yet may never be reality. Father, I need your strength to stop this. Fixing something means repairing it and making it useful again. Help me "fix" my thoughts . . . lock them in . . . anchor them on your truth.

Help me keep my thoughts on things that are positive and good. Help me remember that you have a handle on everything and that you love me more than I can imagine. All things in my life come from you. I commit to praising you every day, reminding myself of your love, care, and goodness. Help me to keep my thoughts firmly on just this day—not troubles from the past, not worries about the future. Today. This day I fix my thoughts on you and your goodness, power, strength, and love. Only then will I know your peace.

Fix your thoughts on what is true, and honorable, and right, and pure, and lovely, and admirable. Think about things that are excellent and worthy of praise. Keep putting into practice all you learned and received from me—everything you heard from me and saw me doing. Then the God of peace will be with you.

Philippians 4:8–9

45

My Waymaker

My loving Lord,
You are my guiding, providing, always present Father. When life becomes confusing, painful, and even frightening (as it often does), I realize that while you may not change the situation I'm facing or remove the problem, you will never leave me to muddle through it alone. You are my Waymaker. Each step I take, I sense your arm around my shoulder and your hand guiding me. I hear your voice whispering words of presence, encouragement, comfort, support, and wisdom.

As I hold tightly to you, Father, this struggle and pain allows me to see your presence and work in my life more clearly than ever. I know this pain is birthing a deeper, stronger, more trusting faith in you. Labor pains that will lead me to a faith like I've never known before. I long for that personal, intimate relationship with you, Father. I yearn for it.

So, through the hard days, pain-filled nights, lonely hours, and frightening minutes, I will take deep breaths and hold tightly to your promises. I am *not* alone. And when I stumble away from that trust, I ask you to pull me back. Remind me that you are growing me and teaching me because you love me. Birth is not easy, but a faith-filled life is worth it.

Haven't I commanded you? Strength! Courage! Don't be timid; don't get discouraged. GOD, your God, is with you every step you take.

Joshua 1:9 The Message

46

Help Us Remember Whose We Are

Holy Father,
I pray for us . . . your people . . . your church. I pray that your Holy Spirit will fill each of us with wisdom and the discernment to separate truth from untruth. I pray that you will guide our minds and hearts to be true to you. Help us to see where we have strayed from your truth and from representing you in love to those around us. Free us from corruption and from believing the lies of the enemy.

Father, fill us with love for you, love for one another, and an urgent concern for those who do not know you. Help us to be solutions to problems by the way we live and not problem makers by our actions and words.

Remind us that you have called us and equipped us to be your disciples. You have given us your Word to teach and guide us, and you have filled us with your Holy Spirit to challenge and correct us.

Oh God, may we be true to you and may we serve you well in these difficult days.

Do not conform to the pattern of this world, but be transformed by the renewing of your mind. Then you will be able to test and approve what God's will is—his good, pleasing and perfect will.

Romans 12:2 NIV

47

Responding to Unkind Words

Dear Father,

I remember the saying from my childhood, "Sticks and stones may break my bones, but words will never hurt me." I remember it, but it isn't really true, is it? Ugly, critical words hurt. Especially ugly words from a loved one or a friend. Unkind, judgmental, accusatory words lay on my heart like bricks. I can't seem to get past them or the feelings they created. An apology helped some, but didn't take away the sense that those words expressed honest feelings that had been suppressed for a while . . . deep-in-the-gut opinions.

Oh God, I pray that these words, the accusations, the judgments, the ugliness hurled at me, are not true. *But* if they are and I've been blinded to my behavior, show me, God. Show me the truth about me so I can be better . . . kinder, more honest, more unselfish, more loving. Just better. Help me know what words to believe and what words to forget. And Father, help me forgive when needed, correct when needed, and never, ever seek revenge.

My dear friends, you should be quick to listen and slow to speak or to get angry.

James 1:19 CEV

48

Taking Responsibility for My Problems

Dear loving Father,

I so often come to you asking for—well, nearly demanding—your help in my life. I arrogantly ask you to bless the choices, actions, and plans I've already made. I ask for your guidance, even though I've already made up my mind. I complain about the problems I face, expecting you to fix them. Father, I do want your wisdom and intercession in my life and in the lives of those

I care about, but I have a confession to make: I ask you for so very much, including your forgiveness; however, I seldom take the time or make the effort to confess my sins to you. I just don't think about the many times I've failed you or disappointed you. I fail to take responsibility for how my own behavior or words or actions may have actually caused my problems and difficulties. I take your forgiveness for granted.

Oh God, I want all the good you give me in life. I gladly receive all your blessings. But I fail to do my part in obeying you by not confessing or repenting of my behavior. I'm sorry, Father. Right now I confess this to you, and I repent of this behavior. I commit to confessing before asking anything of you. Thank you, Father, for second, third, and fourth opportunities to learn and do better.

If we confess our sins, he is faithful and just to forgive us our sins and to cleanse us from all unrighteousness.

1 John 1:9 ESV

49

My Place of Protection

Almighty Father,
You are my protection and my hiding place. I find strength only in you when I'm too weak and fearful to stand on my own. I find protection in you—the only one who can protect me when it feels like my life is imploding. Even though I believe in your loving protection, too often I'm afraid. That's because I get lost in my own head and forget your words of love and promises of care.

Father, take away the fear that consumes my heart. Take away this feeling of resignation that things will never be good again. Oh God, I know that each time I cry out for your help, you answer, so why do I continue to doubt? You're always with me, and you already know what I'm going through. When troubles are overwhelming and terrifying, I do believe you will cover me, protecting me like a parent does a child.

Thank you for that care and deep, deep love. Thank you for being all I could possibly want or need. Help me to always remember that your strength, power, love, and protection are mine.

This I declare about the LORD:
He alone is my refuge, my place of safety;
he is my God, and I trust him.

Psalm 91:2

50

Forgiveness

Oh God,

I've messed up big time. I hurt someone I really care about. I let unkind, critical words spew from my lips. I didn't actually mean them, but I said them. I knowingly spread stories about her that I *knew* were lies. Why did I do that? How can my friend ever forgive me? How can anyone ever trust me again? How do I even forgive myself? I'm sorry, Lord. I really am. I don't even know why I said what I said.

Father, first I ask your forgiveness. I ask you to forgive my jealousy of my friend and my vengeful effort to hurt someone I care about.

I ask you to forgive that I denied saying what I had in fact said. I ask you to help me do better . . . be better.

Please help my friend forgive me, even though I don't deserve it. I understand it will take a long time for her to trust me again, but I pray that she will be able to do so one day.

Last, Father, help me forgive myself. I'm disappointed in myself and spend a lot of time beating myself up. So help me accept your forgiveness and move forward. Thank you, Father. Thank you.

I confessed all my sins to you
and stopped trying to hide my guilt.
I said to myself, "I will confess my
rebellion to the LORD."
And you forgave me! All my guilt is
gone.

Psalm 32:5

51

Provision

Dear Father,

When I'm worried about not having what I need—I don't mean not having what I want but just what I need—I remember that you have always taken care of me. I'm tempted to worry about paying my bills and having medicine, food, and clothes, along with things I don't really need even though I think I do.

But Father, I'm stepping back from worry to just say thank you. Thank you for caring about the multitude of things that worry me. Thank you for understanding when I worry rather than trust you. Thank you for taking care of what I need, often in ways I never would have imagined. Thank you that sometimes you provide what I want even though I don't need it. Thank you for protecting me, guiding me, having a plan for my days. Thank you for always being with me. Thank you for listening to my prayers and even encouraging me to talk with you.

Thank you, Father, that you are all I need and that when I focus on you, all my worries, cares, and fears just fade away.

You can be sure that God will take care of everything you need, his generosity exceeding even yours in the glory that pours from Jesus.

Philippians 4:19 The Message

52

Stopping the Judging Monster

Father,

I must confess something to you . . . something that is creating much stress in my life. I confess that I am very critical of other people. Without even really thinking about it, the thoughts that come into my mind are not generally kind, accepting, or compassionate. Father, why do I immediately go to critical, judgmental thoughts? And why do I speak those thoughts aloud to others? Why do I feel I have the right to judge others or expect them to behave and believe as I do? Why do I have the arrogance to behave with such unkindness toward them?

Father, I don't want to be this way. I want to be known as a loving, kind woman. I want to be a reflection of your love to those around me. There must be a way to do that without compromising my beliefs. Show me how, please. Guide my thoughts, my words, and my actions. Help me remember to treat others as I would like to be treated.

Don't bad-mouth each other, friends. It's God's Word, his Message, his Royal Rule, that takes a beating in that kind of talk. You're supposed to be honoring the Message, not writing graffiti all over it. God is in charge of deciding human destiny. Who do you think you are to meddle in the destiny of others?

James 4:11–12 The Message

53

My Good Shepherd

Dear God,

I am so thankful that you are my shepherd—the one who leads, guides, protects, and provides for me. When I quiet my mind and heart and listen for your voice, I hear you speak and I trust that your words are giving the wisdom I need to hear. I believe, Father, that you will guide my steps and protect me from danger, though not from problems. You give me everything I need in life, from wisdom, protection, and guidance to provision and blessing, though you don't give me everything I *think* I need.

Thank you that you tell me when to stop scurrying around and just rest. Thank you for providing those respites from busyness and problems. Help me to know your voice and to hear it through the blaring noises around me. Help me to know you so well that your voice stands out from all others.

Father, it is a moment-by-moment choice to intentionally trust your leadership and guidance, to know that, like a shepherd protecting his sheep, you are always watching out for me and providing for me. Thank you for always knowing what's best for me and for loving me so deeply.

The Lord is my shepherd, I lack nothing.
He makes me lie down in green
pastures,
he leads me beside quiet waters,
he refreshes my soul.
He guides me along the right paths
for his name's sake.

Psalm 23:1–3 NIV

54

Trusting God's Promises

Oh God,

Here I am again at 3:00 a.m. I wake up to worry about so many things, from paying my rent and putting food on my table to my job, relationships, health, and so much more. I am overwhelmed by the struggles I'm facing and it's wearing me out. These are tough times in our city, state, country . . . well, the whole world. Wars, natural disasters, fires, and diseases have all impacted jobs, businesses, and finances. I'm scared. I've cut my budget to the bare minimum, but it isn't enough. I don't know how I'm going to continue to pay my bills. I don't know where help will come from because so many folks are in the same situation. A very scary situation.

Oh God, I humbly ask for your help, for your provision. I'm not asking to be wealthy; I just want to meet my obligations through a job with a salary that meets my needs. I trust you, God. I don't know how you're going to help me here, but I trust that you will. I know you see where I am. I know you care. I know that nothing is impossible with you. So, each time this 3:00 a.m. wake-up happens, I will remind myself of your promises, your love, your power, and your plan, and that I can trust you. Thank you for your promises. Thank you for your love.

When I am afraid,
   I keep on trusting you.
I praise your promises!
I trust you and am not afraid.
            Psalm 56:3–4 CEV

55

Attitude Change

Oh Father,

I'm sorry, but I get really buried in dealing with my circumstances. The struggle. The worry. The pain. And sometimes . . . I confess . . . the hopelessness. I just don't see how things can ever get better. I feel like I'm losing ground every day. Yet I realize that when I say there's no hope, I'm actually saying that you can't handle this mess. I'm saying that it's bigger than you, and that's why it's hopeless. I confess that by my attitude I'm dismissing your power and strength and even your love for me. I'm allowing hopelessness to take over my life. I recognize that I need an attitude change, Father.

I'm starting that change by praising you because praise reminds me how awesome you are. I praise you for your love and care for me. I praise you for your power and strength. I praise you that nothing is greater than you are. I praise you that you know the end from the beginning. I praise you that the safest place I can be is in your care.

Thank you that spending time praising you takes my focus off my problems and turns my heart toward your goodness and care. It's an attitude changer!

Praise him for his mighty deeds;
praise him according to his excellent
greatness!

Psalm 150:2 ESV

56

Healing a Broken Relationship

Oh God,
My heart is aching because of a broken relationship. You know that I love this person with all my heart. I would not intentionally do anything to hurt her. Whatever happened was unintentional or perhaps a misperception of words or actions. I just don't understand what happened. I want to make it right, but I don't know how.

Father, give me the right words to say to open a conversation. Open my heart to what I've done or said that was hurtful. Give me the compassion and understanding to empathize with her. Open her heart to hear me and be willing to have an open discussion.

Teach me, Father. Teach me to truly care about others and to be patient and understanding with others. Grow my capacity to love deeper. Grow my desire to love as Jesus loves.

Father, give me the courage to admit where I have been wrong and to apologize as I need to. I ask that the relationship with my loved one will be restored and will be even stronger because of this experience. Thank you for your help.

All of you should be of one mind. Sympathize with each other. Love each other as brothers and sisters. Be tenderhearted, and keep a humble attitude.

1 Peter 3:8

57

My New Life Purpose

Father,
I'm going to be really honest here. This stage of life I'm in now is hard. One of the biggest struggles is finding purpose in my life these days. My responsibilities have changed as I've grown older and time has passed. My opportunities have changed too.

But Father, I believe that in this new stage of life, you still have a purpose for me. I had gotten comfortable with the ways I spent my time and was of service to you. So now, help me to be open to your guidance and direction as you lead me to new and different opportunities. It's kind of scary to start new things, and it's definitely hard, but I still want to serve you and serve others. Father, I don't want to just float through the rest of my life. I do want my days to count for you and be useful to your kingdom. Don't let me get lazy, Father. Keep me from settling into apathy. Guide me to purpose in new things. Give me courage to step into them.

Thank you that I'm not through serving you until I step into your heaven.

We humans keep brainstorming options and plans,
but GOD's purpose prevails.

Proverbs 19:21 The Message

58

Working on Me

Oh God,

The work I need to put in to improve my circumstances is overwhelming. It's too much. I'm tempted to gloss over it by not giving it my full attention or my hardest effort. That way I can get through it and move on. Except I know from previous experience that if this work is worth doing, it's worth doing well. I know that if I settle for doing it halfway, I'll regret it in the future. In fact, I will probably have to work even harder to improve the situation then because of the half effort I put in today.

The old saying that if something is worth doing, it's worth doing well is true. Father, give me the perseverance to put in the effort even though I'm tired. Grant me the courage to work on circumstances, relationships, and myself, even when the tasks seem big. Give me the desire to be the best woman I can be and to improve everything about myself so that I can be most reflective of you. That's going to take some work, so grant me your wisdom, discernment, and perseverance to know how to move forward.

I know, Father, that in the end, the results will be worth it. I look forward to the growth and improvements to come.

Throw off your old sinful nature and your former way of life, which is corrupted by lust and deception. Instead, let the Spirit renew your thoughts and attitudes.

Ephesians 4:22–23

59

Letting Go
of Hurt

Father,

I'm carrying around a lot of hurt these days. Hurt, frustration, and yes, even anger. It's eating me up inside. It seems as though the others involved in the situation causing me such angst are doing just fine, and their lives are moving forward. They don't even seem to care. So why can't I let it go? Why do I replay conversations in my mind? Why do I think about what their motives were or question why they said or did things that hurt me so?

Father, I do recognize my responsibility in what happened. At least, I think I do. I've tried to apologize, and my words have been received, but the relationships are still broken . . . and the hurt is still there. Father, help me stop thinking about this constantly.

Help me let go of the hurt and the anger. I know I won't be able to move forward until I can do the letting go, and I know I can't let go without your help. Give me the strength to re-direct my thoughts when this situation comes to mind. Help me look forward to new opportunities, new relationships, and new purpose in my life. Father, don't let this one situation define me.

Thank you for giving me your strength, guidance, and love.

If you are tired from carrying heavy burdens, come to me and I will give you rest.

Matthew 11:28 CEV

60

Comforting Presence

Dear Father,

I want to thank you for the friends and loved ones who come sit with me when I am in pain. I appreciate the warmth, care, and comfort of their presence. I appreciate that they don't feel they need to have answers or even the "right" words to say. These dear ones refrain from lecturing or sharing their thoughts about what I should have done or even pointing out what I did wrong. They recognize the encouragement they give by just being with me.

I know these dear ones are gifts from you. They're responding to the nudges of your Spirit to minister to me. They are being "Jesus with skin on" to me. They give of their time and energy and allow their hearts to care for me. Thank you for placing them in my life. Thank you for their obedience to you. Thank you for the example of your love and care that they are to me. It would be much more painful and difficult to get through hard times if I didn't have these people with me. I am so grateful!

Dear friends, let us love one another, for love comes from God. Everyone who loves has been born of God and knows God.

1 John 4:7 NIV

61

The Woman You Made Me to Be

Oh Father,

I'm losing confidence in myself. I've failed so often. I've disappointed myself, and I'm sure there have been many times when you've been disappointed in me as well. Too often I've failed in efforts to serve you either because I've gotten annoyed with others or because I've lost my temper or become totally self-focused, thinking life is all about me. Too often I've walked away from situations that I know you directed me to, usually because the work just seemed too challenging or too time consuming or even hopeless. I have stopped trusting my ability to discern situations or the motives of people. It's hard to even trust my ability to do things I've done a hundred times before!

Oh God, what's happening? Have I let Satan infiltrate my heart and mind? Is he the one causing these negative thoughts? Am I denying the value of your creation . . . *me* . . . by giving in to these thoughts and denying my own worth?

Please forgive me, Father. Everything you create is good and that includes me. Yes, I fail once in a while, but my heart's desire is to be of use to you and to honor you by how I treat others and how I serve you. Restore my confidence and my belief that I can be the woman you created me to be.

Each time he said, "My grace is all you need. My power works best in weakness." So now I am glad to boast about my weaknesses, so that the power of Christ can work through me.

2 Corinthians 12:9

62

Concern for All

Father,
Today I pray for myself and my fellow believers around the world. We need you to speak into our hearts more than ever, Father. Hold us accountable to the absolute truth of your Word. Guard our hearts against the mixed messages being spoken these days, even by those who claim to be explaining your words but somehow have them a little skewed. Give us wisdom and discernment as we listen for your Spirit's guidance in understanding.

Father, give each of us the ability to proclaim your truth and live in that truth and to do so without disrespecting others or behaving in ways that will push them farther from you rather than draw them to you. This is hard. Maybe harder than it's ever been. But it's also more important than ever, as our world seems to be spiraling away from you.

Help us, Father. Help us be part of your solution. Give us an urgency to be your women, your servants, and examples of your love and concern for all to know you.

The wisdom from above is first of all pure. It is also peace loving, gentle at all times, and willing to yield to others. It is full of mercy and the fruit of good deeds. It shows no favoritism and is always sincere.

James 3:17

63

Light a Fire in Me

Oh God,

I pray today for a fire in my soul. I pray for renewed passion in my relationship with you. I confess that I've settled into a sense of entitlement to your blessings. That makes me lazy about appreciating all you do for me. I'm embarrassed that I've come to expect rather than be grateful for what you do for me, give me, bless me with. I'm so sorry, God. I don't want to be apathetic in my faith. So I ask you to give me a smack-in-the-face reality check to understand my sin of apathy and entitlement and a fresh understanding of your amazing grace in loving me, forgiving me, and blessing me.

Oh God, do not let me take even one moment for granted. I pray for a renewed hunger for your Word. I ask for a constant awareness of your presence in my life and a fresh longing to spend time with you. I pray that my love for you will grow deeper and stronger. I pray that love for you and others will powerfully and energetically motivate my actions, my words, and my intentions in living for you. Oh God, give me an urgency to be a powerful instrument of discipleship for you.

The apostles said to the Lord, "Increase our faith!"

Luke 17:5 NIV

64

You Are My Everything

My loving Father,
You are everything to me. In the foggy cloudiness of my mind today, your sunlight shines. In the tall weeds I'm plodding through, you make a pathway. In my discouragement, you are hope. In my confusion, you offer discernment. In my unknowing, you give wisdom. In my guilt, you are forgiveness. In my lostness, you are love. In my weakness, you give strength. In my defeat, you give victory. In my grief, you give comfort. In my woundedness, you bring healing. In my

weariness, you give rest. In my sin, you give salvation.

You are my salvation. You are my Savior. You guide my steps. You guide my thoughts. You direct my words. You give me the promise of eternity. No power can stand against you. No army is greater than yours. Nothing can separate me from you. You fight for me. You protect me. You love me more than I can imagine. You are truly everything to me.

I pray that you, being rooted and established in love, may have power, together with all the Lord's holy people, to grasp how wide and long and high and deep is the love of Christ, and to know this love that surpasses knowledge—that you may be filled to the measure of all the fullness of God.

Ephesians 3:17–19 NIV

65

Getting Serious

Father,

I've reached a new low . . . when life gets tough, I give up instead of trusting you. It feels like problems are piling on top of problems lately, and I can't get my head above water. Life feels like one of those carnival games where you bop one thing down and something else pops up. One situation raises its ugly head, and I pray and give it to you. Then just as I say amen, something else pops up. Soon there are several things whirling in my mind, and I'm flat-out worried.

I'm tired of dealing with things. I'm tired of struggling to trust you. I'm weary of my faith being so weak. I am drawing a line in the sand today, God. It's time to get totally serious about trusting you and believing you love me and my loved ones and that you will see us through these troubles.

The groundwork, Father, is believing that you are who you say you are—God. You love me. Your Word tells me so. You see the end from the beginning of all situations for all of us, and you have a plan. You will not let me go. Even if things don't go the way I'd like, you are working out your plan for the big picture of my life and the lives of my loved ones. I will choose to believe these things every day. I'm serious about loving and trusting you.

Everyone who honors your name
   can trust you,
because you are faithful
   to all who depend on you.

Psalm 9:10 CEV

66

Minimizing Christ's Sacrifice

Oh Father,

My heart is broken and it's because of me! I'm upset because of the way I've been treating you. I confess that I've been living every day as if my life were totally my own. I am often negligent about spending time in your Word. I've lost my passion for it. I've neglected talking with you. I've begun doubting whether you care to hear what I have to say. I'm stubborn about submitting to your will because I foolishly feel

I know what's best for me. Then, to top it all off, I justify my disobedience and fail to call it sin. I live as though the world owes me things.

Oh God, I'm sorry. Please forgive me. The way I've been behaving takes the sacrifice of Christ so lightly as to believe it cost you nothing. Forgive me for minimizing his suffering and death. Forgive me for ignoring his sacrifice. Forgive me for not appreciating that he covered my sins. Because of him my heart is cleansed. Because of him I can know you.

I'm sorry. I want to start new right now. Thank you for grace. Thank you for forgiveness. Thank you for second chances.

---

*Christ carried the burden
    of our sins.
He was nailed to the cross,
so we would stop sinning
    and start living right.
By his cuts and bruises
    you are healed.*

1 Peter 2:24 CEV

67

Reflecting God's Love

My Father,
Today I pray for better eyesight—the kind that overlooks the negative things in others and instead sees the best in them. I ask for eyes to see intentions that are good over behavior that may not be thoughtful or considerate. I ask that my improved eyesight will be enhanced by a tender heart that's willing to forgive. A heart that doesn't hold grudges but willingly lets go of the urge to get revenge when hurt.

I pray for a softened heart that has compassion on those who are hurting and that looks for ways to help and serve others. I ask that my heart and mind will be guided away from negative thoughts and silent arguments with those who have no idea we are arguing. Keep my mind, heart, and eyes focused on you, Father. Remind me that you forgive me for so many, many things every single day. Help me to pass that forgiveness and grace along to others as I strive to live like Jesus.

Father, never let me forget that others may be able to see you by my attitudes, words, and actions. May I be a good reflection of who you are and how you love.

Watch what God does, and then you do it, like children who learn proper behavior from their parents. Mostly what God does is love you. Keep company with him and learn a life of love. Observe how Christ loved us. His love was not cautious but extravagant. He didn't love in order to get something from us but to give everything of himself to us. Love like that.

Ephesians 5:1–2 The Message

68

Seeking God's Guidance

Oh God,

I don't know what to do. Advice is being thrown at me from all directions. All of it seems good in some ways, but . . . I'm just confused. People I respect have differing opinions, and some of them feel quite strongly that I should do what they say.

But Father, while I do want to honor my mentors and friends, what I truly want is to do your will. Please guide my thoughts. Give me peace in the midst of the cacophony of words, advice, and instructions being offered to me. Father help me to discern your voice. I want to do what you direct me to do. I know that will be best for me and for all others too. I trust you to guide me, even away from my own self-centered desires. I know that what you say will be best. Help me listen for your voice. Direct my thoughts, my steps, my words.

And be in my plans. If I start to wander from your will, draw me back, Father. Keep me right in the palm of your hand. It's the safest place to be.

Trust in the LORD with all your heart;
do not depend on your own
understanding.
Seek his will in all you do,
and he will show you which path to
take.

Proverbs 3:5–6

69

A Life of Praise

My Father,

I confess that too often my prayers are little more than instructions for what I want you to do for me. I'm grateful that I can tell you what's on my heart and even give you my laundry list of wants and needs. But I'm embarrassed that I ask so much yet neglect praising you for what you do for me every day. Oh Lord, I'm sorry for that. I'm sorry for my lack of gratitude and praise.

I want to praise you right now for your blessings and your goodness to me. I praise you for your faithful, loving care for me. I praise you for the blessings of work, home, friends, family, and health. I praise you for the beautiful world you created for me to enjoy. I praise you for my church family and the fellowship of praise we share. I praise you for your Word and the guidance and joy I find through it. I join all of creation in praising you, Lord. May all the earth acknowledge your power, strength, creativity, and love and celebrate that you are the Ruler of all. I praise you. I honor you. I love you. I join my fellow believers in praising you—my loving, generous, forgiving, grace-filled God.

Let everything that has breath praise the Lord!
Praise the Lord!

Psalm 150:6 ESV

70

Help My Failing Faith

Oh God,

Sometimes I really struggle to believe. Doubts overwhelm the knowledge that you love me. I question whether you hear my prayers. I feel so far from you . . . so disconnected. It would be so easy to just walk away. I am tempted to live my life on my own without considering you or what you may want for me. It is a temptation, but . . . I can't do it.

Where else can I turn but to you? I know in my mind that you are real and present and that you do care for me. I know that is true, even if I don't feel the truth of that love right now. There is no one and nothing else to put my trust in. There is no one else who can care for me like your Word promises you do.

So, Father, take away my doubts. Strengthen the small faith I have. Help me, Father. Draw me closer to you. Let me sense your love and care. Help me, please.

Hurry with your answer, GOD!
I'm nearly at the end of my rope.
Don't turn away; don't ignore me!
That would be certain death.
If you wake me each morning with the
sound of your loving voice,
I'll go to sleep each night trusting in
you.
Point out the road I must travel;
I'm all ears, all eyes before you.

Psalm 143:7–8 The Message

71

Submitting to God

Dear God,

I've had enough. I have decided that I've had enough of trying to run my own life and doing everything the way I want. It hasn't been working so well for me, and yet I've persisted in doing it anyway. I confess that the things I have thought were super important may not have actually been the major issues I've supposed them to be. By trying to run my life myself, I've hurt people I care about. I've neglected people I could have helped. I've spent way too much time focusing on me and what I want without considering what you might want for me. Because of that, I've been disobedient, controlling, and not submissive to you.

Today I'm turning away from negative thoughts and behaviors. From this day on, I will intentionally seek your guidance. I promise you that I will regularly read your Word. I will pray. I will be silent and listen for your guidance. Oh my Father, I yearn to follow you and obey you. Please help me with this resolution.

So humble yourselves under the mighty power of God, and at the right time he will lift you up in honor.

1 Peter 5:6

72

Praying God's Love for Others

Father,

Someone I love very much is really suffering. It seems like one thing after another has happened to her, and she just can't get her head above water. Financial problems, relationship issues, work problems, and over and over again she faces health struggles. Why do some people have so much to deal with while others seem to just slide through life? I don't understand.

I bring this dear one before you, God. I ask you for healing in her body and soul. Restore her health. Comfort her. Encourage her. Remind her that you are with her and she is never, ever alone. I pray that she will sense your presence in a more powerful way than she ever has. God, I pray that by your grace she will have an oasis of peace for a while. I pray that in that time of peace, her spirit will begin to heal and the bruises on her heart to fade away. Give her joy deep in her soul by your presence with her. Remind her that you love her more than she can conceive and that nothing can change that love. Remind her also that she has friends who love her deeply and pray for her daily. Thank you, Lord, for your deep, deep love.

The LORD your God is in your midst,
a mighty one who will save;
he will rejoice over you with gladness;
he will quiet you by his love;
he will exult over you with loud singing.

Zephaniah 3:17 ESV

73

God Gives More Grace

Father,

I am so very thankful for your grace. It is by your grace that you forgive my failures, see my heart, and know that I honestly do yearn to know you more deeply and serve you more fully. But, oh God, I fail so often. Still, you never give up on me. I'm so thankful that your grace grows even more deeply in my heart when I humbly submit to your will and let go of my efforts at controlling my life and your work. It's hard to let go, but your grace gives me second, third, and fourth opportunities to do better, obey you more fully, serve you more seriously, and love to the greatest degree. Your grace gives me your very best. I know that I don't deserve any of it. That's what makes your love and grace so amazing. What a blessing. None of the good things in my life are deserved, and there is nothing I can do to earn them. You give me so much simply because of your love for me and desire to know me more deeply. Thank you, Father.

He gives us more grace. That is why Scripture says:

> *"God opposes the proud*
>   *but shows favor to the humble."*

James 4:6 NIV

74

Failure Isn't the End

Dear God,

I feel like such a disappointment. I really do. I'm disappointed in myself, so I know I must disappoint you too. I try so hard to live in obedience to you, to honor you by my life, to be a positive reflection to all but . . . I fail. I'm not consistent. I give in to temptation so easily. My selfishness flies out so easily. Oh God, I wonder, how can I ever be of use to you when my faith walk is so inconsistent?

But then I remember the reports of people in the Bible who struggled and failed—from

Moses, Noah, and David to the woman at the well who had five failed marriages—and you still had great love for them, compassion for them, and responsibilities for them! They had work to do for you, and they did it! Thank you for including their stories in Scripture. They are an incredible encouragement to me because they remind me that failure isn't forever. A messed-up past doesn't mean a hopeless future. I'm so thankful!

So now there is no condemnation for those who belong to Christ Jesus. And because you belong to him, the power of the life-giving Spirit has freed you from the power of sin that leads to death.

Romans 8:1–2

75

Truth,
Not Feelings

Dear God,

You know where my faith gets stuck? I do. I put way too much emphasis on how I'm feeling about things. If I go for a few days without feeling your love or care, then I begin to doubt what I know to be true—what your Word tells me is true. I guess that opens a doorway for Satan to come in and whisper all sorts of untrue things about you, doesn't it?

I've heard dozens of times that I shouldn't put too much emphasis on feelings. The hard thing is that I'm human . . . and female . . . so feelings are kind of always right at the surface. When I get discouraged, I ignore the obvious ways your love is present and only look for the "big" miracles or things I want you to do.

Father, help me remember that I must not put more value on my feelings than I do on your Word. When I get discouraged by what I feel, please bring the truths I know from Scripture to my memory. The verses I've read over and over, highlighted, memorized, and believed. Help me to focus on truth, not on feelings. I trust the truth of your Word.

Every part of Scripture is God-breathed and useful one way or another—showing us truth, exposing our rebellion, correcting our mistakes, training us to live God's way. Through the Word we are put together and shaped up for the tasks God has for us.

2 Timothy 3:16–17 The Message

76

The Way of Salvation

Father,
I need your help. Here's the thing: I believe with all my heart that true faith in Jesus is the one and only way to know you, to be rescued from my sin, to know the power of your love and strength in my life, to be saved from an eternity separated from you. I believe that Jesus is the only way. I want to share that with people who don't yet know about your love. I want to be true to the truth of your Word. The problem is knowing how to present this truth in a manner

that doesn't push away people who have a different belief system. I know I risk offending them by stating what I know to be true. So, how do I present truth without having them walk away in disgust? I can only do so through the power, wisdom, and discernment of your Spirit working in my life.

Teach me. Guide my timing in speaking. Guide my words, the tone of my voice, and the way I present truth. I don't want to compromise truth, but I long for all to know you. Please help me, Father. Help me share that Jesus is the only way.

Jesus said to him, "I am the way, and the truth, and the life. No one comes to the Father except through me."

John 14:6 ESV

77

Taking Responsibility for Me

My Father,

Forgive me. Please forgive me. I have been so very quick to criticize and make judgments about others for their attitudes, their words, and their actions. I guess I feel that everyone should think and behave as I do. That in itself is very arrogant, like I think I'm always right, which of course I'm not. I am so quick to judge others' behaviors, when in reality my own actions are often worse than theirs.

Please forgive me. Father, help me remember that I only need to take care of me—my thoughts, attitudes, words, and actions. I'm responsible for me. I should not be judging others or giving them guidance and unrequested advice when my own life needs cleaning up. I don't want to be hypocritical in my faith, Father. Help me to be honest in my assessment of my own life and to be loving and supportive of others while offering advice and prayer when it's requested.

Why do you look at the speck of sawdust in your brother's eye and pay no attention to the plank in your own eye? . . . You hypocrite, first take the plank out of your own eye, and then you will see clearly to remove the speck from your brother's eye.

Matthew 7:3, 5 NIV

78

Praying with Thanksgiving

Dear Father,

I don't take lightly the fact that you want me to pray. I try to come to you about everything that's on my heart and mind. I pray about the things I'm worried about. I pray about situations that scare me. I want your help with decisions I must make. I pray for the needs and problems of my loved ones. I'm continuously amazed not only that you hear my prayers but that you encourage me to pray. What a blessing that is, especially when I'm really worried or scared, like I am today.

I'm scared about how a situation can possibly be resolved. I'm worried. But even though I'm nervous, I've realized something. Today I read Colossians 4:2 and I was immediately stricken with guilt that I seldom take time to thank you for hearing my prayers. Not just for hearing them but for calming me as I pray, and also for answering my prayers.

Thank you for hearing me. Thank you for caring about what I care about. Thank you that as I'm talking to you, my soul calms. Being in your presence is like a gentle salve for my aching heart. Thank you for working out your will in every circumstance. Thank you that you know what's best for me and those I love. Thank you for the privilege of prayer.

Continue steadfastly in prayer, being watchful in it with thanksgiving.

Colossians 4:2 ESV

79

Right Priorities

Dear Father,

The words from Galatians 6:8 just pierce my heart because I have to admit that I'm guilty of just what they say. Oh Father, I have been lax in spending time with you, and now I have lost my way and focused my attention and energy on pursuing things that I *think* will make me happy. People and things that seem so wonderful that they will surely be satisfying for me. But they aren't, at least not for long. Spending so much time on those things keeps me from spending time with you, which of course is where I will truly find satisfaction!

Father, does it make you sad that I'm making something more important to me than you are? I'm sorry and I confess this to you. Reading in your Word that I'm decaying my very soul by doing this frightens me. I ask you to help me have the strength to turn away from this behavior. Father, show me when I'm doing it and help me be intentional in turning away from it.

Give me the urgency and passion to long to focus my attention on knowing you and serving you.

Those who live only to satisfy their own sinful nature will harvest decay and death from that sinful nature. But those who live to please the Spirit will harvest everlasting life from the Spirit.

Galatians 6:8

80

God and God Alone

Oh God,

I feel scared and lost. It feels like I'm wandering in thick darkness. I'm facing things I've never had to face before. I have important decisions to make that are confusing. I don't know what tomorrow will bring. I don't have the strength or wisdom to know how to handle whatever comes. The crutches I've leaned on have been knocked away. I am alone. I have no one to depend on . . . except you.

Maybe that's what I need to focus on—all I have is you . . . and all I need is you. So maybe it's intentional and actually a blessing that people who are friends, advisors, and mentors are simply not available now for various reasons. You, Father, you are all I need. You know that I love you. You know that I trust you. Please, God, protect me from situations and people who aren't good for me. Protect me from myself—my own choices. Remind me that you are holding me in the palm of your hand. Thank you for your love and care.

> Please listen, LORD,
> and answer my prayer!
>   I am poor and helpless.
> Protect me and save me
>   because you are my God.
> I am your faithful servant,
>   and I trust you.
>
>   Psalm 86:1–2 CEV

81

Choosing God over All Else

Dear God,
I choose you. When, all around me, voices are shouting the importance of money, power, success, or fame, I choose you. I choose love. When, all around me, criticism is raging, ugly racist words are shouted, and sarcasm or hatred is aimed at those who choose you, I choose love. I choose kindness. Even when it seems bullies are winning, hatred is growing, and political and religious divides are making people ugly, I choose kindness. I choose hu-

mility. Even when it appears that pride, power, and arrogance are the norm, I choose humility. I choose purity. Even though our culture has turned to sex, drugs, and immorality, I choose purity. I choose honesty. Even when self-promotion, dishonesty, and financial gain at all costs are more normal, I choose honesty.

I choose all these things because I choose you. I intentionally choose to follow you, serve you, obey you, and love you because I know, believe, and trust that you love me, have saved me, and have a future for me.

My dear brothers and sisters, be strong and immovable. Always work enthusiastically for the Lord, for you know that nothing you do for the Lord is ever useless.

1 Corinthians 15:58

82

The End of Grief

My loving Father,

My heart is breaking. I've just lost someone who was so very dear to me. I prayed so sincerely and so long for her healing. I trusted you to heal her. I believed you would. But you didn't. At least, not in the way I wanted you to. Of course, I know she's with you now. I get that. And I know that's a good thing for her. Selfishly, I wanted her to stay here. I wanted her in my life.

Now I have this gaping hole in my heart— a hole she used to fill. I shall miss her. I shall miss the conversation, the laughter, the shared tears, the wisdom of her advice. My life will be emptier without her presence. Thank you for letting me have her in my life for a while.

But now I need your comfort. I need to be reminded that you can fill the void her passing has left. I long for your comfort. I yearn to know that you understand. Help me know that you heard my prayers but that your plan was better to bring her to heaven rather than leave her here.

I need you right now, Father. I need you more than I ever have before. Show me that this pain will one day be over.

He will wipe away every tear from their eyes, and death shall be no more, neither shall there be mourning, nor crying, nor pain anymore, for the former things have passed away.

Revelation 21:4 ESV

83

Accepting
God's Plans

Father,

I confess that I'd like my story to be different.

When I was younger, I had hopes and dreams of how my life would turn out . . . I'd have a nice house, a career, fulfillment, success. Very little of my life has turned out the way I'd planned. Now here I am on the downhill side of life, and the possibilities for many of those dreams are in the rearview mirror, lost in the dust of the road I've traveled. So yes, I wish some things could have turned out differently . . . but they didn't. And you know what? That's okay. I am learning to let go of what could have been and accept what is for one reason and one reason only—you.

Father, you are the Waymaker. You have always had a plan for my life, and you have worked it out a step at a time. It hasn't always been easy. It still isn't sometimes. I've been disappointed sometimes. I've been lost sometimes. But, I've always come to the point of accepting what you have for me. In fact, I'm honored to be where I am, doing what I'm doing today, because that is what you want for me.

We can make our own plans,
but the LORD gives the right answer.

Proverbs 16:1

84

Serving
as God Asks

Father,

I think that, without realizing it, I've been taking the easy way out. I have gladly given my tithes and offerings to you, thinking that covered my service to you. I didn't really think about it, but I guess I thought that meant I didn't even need to consider anything that required me to give of my time, energy, or comfort. I thought giving money to your work could even cover the times when I was "too busy" to spend time with you, reading your Word, praying, worshiping, praising. I justified myself with the fact that my busyness was providing more money to give to your work . . . work I didn't feel I needed to actually be physically involved in.

I get it now, Father. While my tithes and offerings are good—needed, even—you want more from me. In fact, you want my whole life—my heart, soul, time, energy, and thoughts. I must be open to do what you ask, go where you ask, serve in whatever way you ask . . . even if I'm frightened or find a situation or a person to be unlikable or distasteful.

You'll give the courage I need. You'll calm my heart. You will equip me to do whatever you ask me to do. Forgive my justifications. Forgive my blindness. Accept my apology and, Father . . . use me in any way you want.

I take joy in doing your will, my God,
for your instructions are written on
my heart.

Psalm 40:8

85

God's Great Love and Mercy

Almighty Father,

There are some days . . . there are some times . . . when I question whether you're even paying attention to what's going on in my life. These are the days when I am consumed with my own struggles and my own pain. Truthfully, these are the days when I need you more than ever, Lord.

I am so very grateful for the calming beauty of the words in Lamentations 3:22–23. What a comfort it is to know that your love *never* ceases. It's always there, even when I can't *feel* it. Nothing can separate me from your love. It's steadfast, immovable, constant. I will hold on to that. And your mercies—oh Lord, I am so thankful for your mercies. The mercy of salvation that changed my day-in-and-day-out life and that promises wonderful hope for my eternity. Your mercies of compassion, kindness, and forgiveness are never ending. Every morning when I open my eyes there are new mercies for that day. You are so faithful to me. Your love and mercy prove that. So, even in the dark times when I feel lost, I will hang on to these truths.

The steadfast love of the Lord never ceases;
his mercies never come to an end;
they are new every morning;
great is your faithfulness.

Lamentations 3:22–23 ESV

86

Courage, Power, and Love

My gracious Father,
I confess that I still struggle with fear sometimes. Even with what I know of you and the
history we share, my reaction is still fear when I
am anxious that people may be critical of what
I think or say. I become very timid and nervous
when the opportunity comes to talk about
you because much of the world is so critical
of those who have faith in you. Fear makes me
. . . quiet. I'd rather be still and let others take
their chances with being criticized or bullied

as they witness for you or take a stand for what is right, fair, and moral according to your Word. I'll willingly stand behind them and nod in agreement. Yet I don't want to be controlled by fear, Father. So I ask you to give me courage. Remind me that your incredible power is available to me. Help me have an urgency to share my faith so that people around me don't miss out on the opportunity to know you and share in your eternity. Give me a love for others that motivates me to share with them and help them in any way I can. Help me be disciplined in knowing what to say and when to speak up. Help me, Father, to be a courageous, strong, love-filled woman for your kingdom.

God has not given us a spirit of fear and timidity, but of power, love, and self-discipline.

2 Timothy 1:7

87

When You Know What to Do—Do It

Oh God,

Confession time for me . . . there have been many times I've known in my heart what I *should* do—what you are asking me to do. But I've let fear or laziness or anxiety or a bazillion other things keep me from doing it. I have become an expert at justifying that I'm too busy or I don't have enough knowledge or someone else is more qualified. I seldom say the truth, which is simply, "I don't want to." I guess I never thought that was actually sin because I felt I had a good excuse, so the statement in James 4:17 just smacks me in the face.

Knowing in my heart the right thing to do in a situation but turning away or just being quiet instead is sin. I'm so sorry, Father. I'm so sorry. Please forgive me and please don't give up on me. I ask you to keep giving me opportunities to do right and prompting me to act. Remind me when I get scared or lazy that disobeying what I know to do is actual, real sin. I don't want to do that.

Remember, it is sin to know what you ought to do and then not do it.

James 4:17

88

God's Comfort and Love for My Friend

Dear God,

Do you hear the silence? It's deafening. My precious loved one has stopped talking, stopped calling, stopped texting, and I really miss her. Her silence reverberates in my heart. I want to help her, but I can't. I hope she's talking with you, Father. I know you hear her prayers. You see her tears. You feel her pain. You know what she's lost. You see the bruises on her heart and the scars in her soul. I miss her, Father. I ache because of the pain I know she's wading through. All I can do these days is pray for her. I know that's the best thing to do, but you understand that I wish I could do more.

Oh Father, let her know you're close—right there with her, walking through the pain with her, holding her close, guiding her steps, picking her up when she stumbles. Comfort her. Encourage her. Father, when she can't find the words to pray, see her heart and know what she needs. Remind her, too, that I'm here. I don't want to push her to talk before she's ready, but I want her to remember that I love her and will always be here for her. Thank you, God, for loving her. I know you love her even more than I do.

If your heart is broken, you'll find GOD
   right there;
if you're kicked in the gut, he'll help you
   catch your breath.

                    Psalm 34:18 The Message

89

Showing Grace to Others

Father,

I confess that sometimes I forget whose daughter I am. I lose sight of the responsibilities you have given me. I ask you to help me remember that how I treat other people, how I interact with them, and how I conduct myself reflect you. I can help draw people to you rather than push them away. It's not always easy to be kind, be patient, and give people the benefit of the doubt when they aren't being kind. I can't do it without your help. I remember, though, that you constantly forgive me for sinning—over and over. You forgive me time after time after time. I need to learn from that and then apply that same kind of mercy and grace to others, even if they aren't sorry for what they've done. Father, please just help me to be a good representative of you by reflecting your grace, mercy, and forgiveness. May your love shine through me to all I meet.

Since God chose you to be the holy people he loves, you must clothe yourselves with tenderhearted mercy, kindness, humility, gentleness, and patience. Make allowance for each other's faults, and forgive anyone who offends you. Remember, the Lord forgave you, so you must forgive others.

Colossians 3:12–13

90

Make Me a Truthful Woman

Dear Father,

In the haste of a moment, or in order to be liked or accepted, I sometimes say things that aren't completely true.

Sometimes I tell a "little" lie and justify it by saying that I'm protecting someone's feelings. Sometimes I lie by what I don't say rather than what I do say, and that's usually because I'm scared of what others will think about me.

Father, I don't want to be a liar. I want to be trustworthy and honest. I ask for your help and guidance in setting filters for my words. Make discernment one filter through which my words pass, meaning if it doesn't need to be said, keep me from speaking. May kindness filter how I speak, because tone and attitude are louder than actual words. Help me have courage to speak up for what's right, honest, and fair. Give me strength to take a stand for those things and especially for you, regardless of what others may say or think. Give me wisdom so that the words I speak are true to you and not just my opinions or feelings.

I pray that my family and friends will know they can trust me to be truthful and filtered with love, kindness, and discernment. I need your help to be all these things, Father.

The LORD hates every liar,
but he is the friend of all
who can be trusted.
Proverbs 12:22 CEV

91

Words and Actions That Match

Loving Father,

I don't want my faith to be only empty words . . . words that do not motivate me to action. Of course, I know all the right things to say . . . all the Christian words. I can talk a good faith and quote lots of Bible verses. And it's not that I don't believe those verses; I do, but I want my faith to be more than words. I want to put feet to my faith so that my actions—how I spend my time, where I put my energy, any attitudes I put forth, and, well, really everything about me—match my words. I long for the kind of faith that makes a difference for your kingdom. I know that change comes from more than just good words. My words must be said in love, kindness, concern, and compassion for others. Please give me more and more opportunities to serve you. Opportunities to show love to others. Chances to sacrificially give of my time and energy. Let my actions prove my words, that living for you, loving you, and loving others are important to me.

Now someone may argue, "Some people have faith; others have good deeds." But I say, "How can you show me your faith if you don't have good deeds? I will show you my faith by my good deeds."

James 2:18

92

True Satisfaction

Father,

I struggle with being satisfied. I confess that too often I give in to the culture's standard of never being satisfied and always striving for more. It's hard to fight the pressure to join in the climb toward more and more and more. I recognize that satisfaction must be based on my life in you, not on what material things I acquire. I've heard too often from the rich and famous that getting more money and more things doesn't fill that void of loneliness. It doesn't help someone be loved for who they are and not for what others can get from them.

True satisfaction comes only from knowing you and the assurance that you are always with me. I am not lonely, Father, because I am not alone. Satisfaction in my days doesn't come from "stuff," like money, fancy cars, bigger houses, or designer clothes. It doesn't come from power, influence, or career success. Father, remind me every day—many times a day—that satisfaction comes from knowing you, obeying you, doing your will, and becoming the woman, family member, and friend you want me to be. Never let me get confused about where true satisfaction comes from.

Don't love money; be satisfied with what you have. For God has said,

> *"I will never fail you.*
> *I will never abandon you."*

Hebrews 13:5

93

What True Love Looks Like

Father God,

The verses in 1 Corinthians 13 that describe love teach me so much and convict me of how I often fail to love others. Forgive me, Father, and help others forgive me, because too often I treat the people I love most with impatience and selfishness. I want them to do what I want, and I want them to think the way I think because I believe my way is the best way. Too often I refuse to listen to any of their ideas or wishes. I push them down in an effort to lift myself up. I get caught up in tooting my own horn as I self-promote. I end up wanting everyone to know how successful I am, how wise, creative, and strong I am. I want them not just to *know* these things but to admire and praise me. As I demand my own way, I become pushy and indignant when others won't listen to me. I admit this is wrong, and I'm sorry for behaving this way.

Father, help me remember what true love looks like. Help me treat the ones I love with a pure love that comes from you, a love that wants the best for them and lifts them up rather than pushes them down.

Love is patient and kind. Love is not jealous or boastful or proud or rude. It does not demand its own way. It is not irritable, and it keeps no record of being wronged.

1 Corinthians 13:4–5

94

Wisdom and Guidance

Oh God,
Sometimes I feel so very lost. I can't see what's ahead for me. I don't know what to do in many situations. I can't find the right thing to do or the right times to speak and keep quiet. It paralyzes me, God. I can go to friends and mentors for advice, and of course I'm thankful for them, but the truth is that oftentimes, they don't know what I should do or which way I should turn either. That's when I am incredibly

thankful that I can come to you. True wisdom comes only from you.

Father, thank you that I can come to you with all my questions, doubts, and fears and with every struggle I have, and you will give me guidance and wisdom. You don't make me feel bad about asking. You don't condemn me for not knowing what to do. You aren't critical when I get lost in the darkness. You know that I learn by asking. You know that my asking means I trust you to guide me in doing what's best for me and in relating to others the best way I can. Thank you for the privilege of coming to you for wisdom and guidance.

If you don't know what you're doing, pray to the Father. He loves to help. You'll get his help, and won't be condescended to when you ask for it. Ask boldly, believingly, without a second thought.

James 1:5–6 The Message

95

The Promise of Heaven

Almighty God,
Thank you for the wonderful promise of heaven. Knowing that heaven is mine for eternity gives me strength to get through some of the hard times I face here in this life. Your sacrificial plan that makes a way for me to be in heaven is absolute proof of your mercy, grace, and incredible love for me. Regardless of how many times I stumble, how many times I doubt, how many times I struggle, I know that

heaven is mine for eternity because of my faith in Jesus.

I can't even begin to imagine the glory of heaven, how beautiful it will be, and what a blessing it will be to actually stand in your presence. Thank you that your promise of my room in your eternal home is secure. Nothing can change that. Anticipating being in your presence fills me with such joy. What an amazing reward to spend eternity with you and fellow believers. Praising you. Loving you. Becoming the fullest version of who you have planned for me to be as the barriers of sinfulness are gone.

Jesus said to his disciples, "Don't be worried! Have faith in God and have faith in me. There are many rooms in my Father's house. I wouldn't tell you this, unless it was true. I am going there to prepare a place for each of you.

John 14:1–2 CEV

96

God Handles My Fear

My powerful Father,

Help! The world is crashing down on me. Everywhere I look, I see problems. People are attacking me—sometimes because of things I've said or what they perceive my intentions to be, sometimes simply because I take a stand for you. I try to stand for what's just, moral, kind, fair, and honest, and some people feel threatened by those stances and attack me for them.

I'm afraid, Father. I'm actually afraid of the enemies around me, attacking with the intent of deep, long-lasting hurt. It's obvious that they want to stop me from standing for you. They want to stop me from working for you. I need you, Father.

I need your encouragement to do the brave things. I need your wisdom and discernment to know when to speak, when to be quiet, and how to frame my comments and attitudes. I ask for your strength and courage to fill my soul. Father, be my protection and shield. Give me confidence that you know what's happening and that you see what my heart's intentions are, even if I don't always carry them out perfectly.

Help me, Father, to trust your promise to shield and protect me. Thank you for that promise. Thank you for your presence. Thank you for saving me from my enemies.

Surely God is my salvation;
I will trust and not be afraid.
The Lord, the Lord himself, is my
strength and my defense;
he has become my salvation.

Isaiah 12:2 NIV

97

Help Your Church

Father,

Today I pray for your church—the worldwide group of Christians who strive to know you, love you, and obey you. I pray for our efforts to share the reality of you with the rest of the world. Father, there are times when the choices some of us make seem to do more harm than good. We need to be careful of how we behave, how we speak, and our attitudes, because those very things may drive people away from you rather than draw them to you. Father, give us all the wisdom to know how to show love to others without compromising the truth of your Word.

It's not always easy, God, to stand for right and maintain an attitude of love. But Father, the world needs you now more than ever. There's so much wickedness and hatred. There are so many perverted ideas being presented as truth. There are things being blamed on you and judgments being made about what you should do or could do "if you really cared." Father, I ask you to fill your people with words and actions that are founded in the absolute truth of your Word. Teach us how to live those truths and share them, couched in love, just as you instructed us to do.

God wants us to grow up, to know the whole truth and tell it in love—like Christ in everything.

Ephesians 4:15 *The Message*

98

Patience and Hope

Oh God,

I confess that patience is not my strong point. When I am struggling with something, I want the hard stuff to be over. I don't enjoy the journey; I want the destination. I'm sorry to say my first reaction when I have trouble is not to rejoice. My first reaction is usually to complain (loudly to anyone who will listen), beg for relief, or give in to depression or fear. Father, I know I should be able to view troubles as opportunities to learn and grow. That's where the patience would come in, as I would willingly go through the hard times, seeking to learn and grow stronger in my faith.

Father, I need to ask you to help me be patient, though it scares me to ask that. I certainly don't want to ask for troubles, but I do want to grow. Remind me of the hope I have because of you—hope that my troubles aren't pointless because through them my faith can grow stronger. Give me the patience to wait for that growth.

And Father, thank you that I can talk with you anytime about my struggles and my fears. You always hear me. You care about what I'm experiencing. You are my hope!

Rejoice in our confident hope. Be patient in trouble, and keep on praying.

Romans 12:12

99

Hating Evil as God Does

Oh God,

Teach me to recognize evil . . . in me and around me . . . and to hate it. I need your help to see the evidence of evil in my own life. I'm so blinded to it sometimes because I too easily justify away my own failures of pride and arrogance. I even claim that I'm obeying you by my pride in what a wonderful spiritual leader I am. That's evil. You say that pride is evil. The other evidence of evil that's too often in my life shows itself in my speech. Oh Father, I can be so unkind in what I say. I can be so critical and judgmental of others. My arrogance and pride come through in how and what I speak. I'm so sorry for my laziness in monitoring what I say and how I say it.

Father, help me to hate evil as you do. Help me to see it in myself and to make every effort to rid my life of the evidence of evil. Fill my heart with love for you and love for others. Help me seek to honor you by how I live and especially by how I treat other people. May my love for you shine brightly as I fight against evil in myself and in the world.

All who fear the LORD will hate evil.
Therefore, I hate pride and arrogance,
corruption and perverse speech.

Proverbs 8:13

100

Celebrating All God Is and Does

Father,

This is what I've learned in my faith journey—to celebrate you in the good times *and* the hard times! I celebrate you when troubles come into my life. I celebrate you when wonderful things happen. I celebrate you in the day-in-and-day-out activities of my life. I celebrate you in the special times of unexpected joy. I celebrate you because you love me. You have chosen to shower me with your grace in forgiveness, and you have given me chance after chance to learn from my failures and grow stronger in my obedience to your Word. Father, I celebrate the privilege of knowing you and serving you. I celebrate that I can bring glory to you by my obedience and service. I celebrate that you have given me life, a home, family, and friends. I celebrate that all I have or ever will have comes from the generosity of your heart and hand. You are good, Father. You are good. Even when life is difficult, I celebrate that you are good. Your love is constant and pure, and nothing can change that. I celebrate you!

Whether you eat or drink, or whatever you do, do it all for the glory of God.

1 Corinthians 10:31

Index of Prayers
by Topic